Simulating Distributional Impacts of Macro-dynamics

OTHER TITLES IN THE ADePT SERIES

Analyzing Food Security Using Household Survey Data: Streamlined Analysis with ADePT Software (2014) by Ana Moltedo, Nathalie Troubat, Michael Lokshin, and Zurab Sajaia

A Unified Approach to Measuring Poverty and Inequality—Theory and Practice: Streamlined Analysis with ADePT Software (2013) by James Foster, Suman Seth, Michael Lokshin, and Zurab Sajaia

Health Equity and Financial Protection: Streamlined Analysis with ADePT Software (2011) by Adam Wagstaff, Marcel Bilger, Zurab Sajaia, and Michael Lokshin

Assessing Sector Performance and Inequality in Education: Streamlined Analysis with ADePT Software (2011) by Emilio Porta, Gustavo Arcia, Kevin Macdonald, Sergiy Radyakin, and Michael Lokshin

For more information about Streamlined Analysis with ADePT software and publications, visit www.worldbank.org/adept.

STREAMLINED ANALYSIS WITH ADePT SOFTWARE

Simulating Distributional Impacts of Macro-dynamics

Theory and Practical Applications

Sergio Olivieri
Sergiy Radyakin
Stainslav Kolenikov
Michael Lokshin
Ambar Narayan
Carolina Sánchez-Páramo

 **WORLD BANK GROUP**

Contents

Contents

Figures

Tables

Contents

Foreword

Economists have long been interested in measuring the poverty and distributional impacts of different kinds of macroeconomic projections based on structural reforms, macroeconomic shocks, and other events. A common solution is to extrapolate the welfare impact of these projections from the historical response of income or consumption poverty to changes in output by estimating an elasticity of poverty to growth. Although this method provides an aggregate estimate, it does not identify those who are likely to be winners and losers of that projection.

The World Bank's Poverty Reduction and Equity Group developed a microsimulation model based on well-known approaches described in the economics literature. This project was undertaken at the request of World Bank staff working abroad, as well as of country governments, in the wake of the 2008–09 global financial crisis. Without good high-frequency micro-level data, which most developing countries lack, this method was still able to provide some guidance to questions such as "How are the impacts shared across the distribution?" and "What are the characteristics of those who would become poor as a consequence of a macroeconomic shock?"

Although conceived with the financial crisis in mind, the model can be applied to any macro event that leads to a change in real output (total and by economic sector) and employment structure (total and by economic sector). To begin, simple macroeconomic projections were used as the "macro linkages" to a micro behavioral model built from household data. The model was then conceptualized, refined, and tested in a diverse mix of countries not only during the financial crisis (such as Bangladesh, Mexico, Mongolia, the Philippines, and Poland), but also after the crisis (such as Armenia, Belarus, Costa Rica, the Kyrgyz Republic, Moldova, Panama, Poland, Serbia, Romania, Ukraine, and Uruguay).

This book provides clear guidance to analysts wanting to implement this microsimulation model. To make the model more accessible to users, the Poverty Reduction and Equity Group and the Development Research Group developed the ADePT Simulation Module. Probably the first of its kind, this software greatly enhances the usability of microsimulations to predict the distributional impact of macroeconomic projections. At the same time, we see this not as an end in itself, but rather as a foundation to build on for the future. As the model is used more frequently, we expect to see further enhancements and refinements that will continue to improve the quality of analyses the World Bank can provide to countries.

The book is organized in two parts. The first part summarizes the method underlying the microsimulation model, provides examples of how outputs can be used, and discusses the method's limitations. It finishes with a comprehensive technical explanation of each estimation step in the simulation process. The second part is a step-by-step guide to implementing the model using the ADePT Simulation Module. Topics range from preparing the macro and micro inputs to the module to interpreting the results and evaluating the usefulness of these outputs for further policy analysis.

Jaime Saavedra Chanduvi
Director, Poverty Reduction
and Equity
Poverty Reduction and Economic
Management
The World Bank

Christina Malmberg Calvo
Acting Director, Poverty Reduction
and Equity
Poverty Reduction and Economic
Management
The World Bank

Acknowledgments

The core team that developed the ADePT Simulation Module consists of Sergio Olivieri (Economist, PRMPR), Stanislav Kolenikov (Consultant, DECCI), and Sergiy Radyakin (Economist, DECCI). The team was supported by valuable contributions from Ambar Narayan (Lead Economist, PRMPR), Carolina Sánchez-Páramo (Sector Manager, ECSP3), Bilal Habib (Consultant, PRMPR), Michael Lokshin (Manager, DECCT), and Zurab Sajaia (Senior Computational Economist, DECCI). The team would like to thank all those who contributed at various stages of the development of the module and the writing of this manual.

The team gratefully acknowledges all those who supported this tool in the regions by introducing it to countries and statistical offices as well as by supporting country and regional hands-on training courses. Special thanks to Samuel Freije (Lead Economist, LCSPR), Ruslan Yemtsov (Lead Economist, HDNSP), Daniela Marotta (Senior Economist, MNSED), Paolo Verme (Senior Economist, MNSED), Kinnon Scott (Senior Economist, LCSPP), Leonardo Lucchetti (Economist, LCSPP), Carlos Rodriguez Castelan (Economist, LCSPP), Maria Ana Lugo (Economist, LCSPP), Hannah Sibylle Nielsen (Senior Economist, LCSPE), Caterina Ruggeri Laderchi (Senior Economist, ECSP3), Alexandru Cojocaru (Economist, ECSP3), Victor Sulla (Senior Economist, AFTP1), and Erwin Tiongson (Senior Economist, LCSPP).

The team is deeply grateful to the reviewers Martin Cicowiez and Francesco Figari for their precise comments which have significantly enriched this book and to William Creitz for his excellent editorial assistance. Very warm thanks to Nelly Obias (Program Assistant, PRMPR) for her hard work and enthusiasm in supporting multiple staff training sessions in World Bank Headquarters, always with a smile.

The team thanks Christina Malmberg (Sector Manager, PRMPR) and Jaime Saavedra (Sector Director, PRMPR) for their unflagging enthusiasm and support and for valuing the relevance of such tools, especially ADePT, that make technical analysis more broadly accessible and bring it closer to informing dialogue and operations.

This project is made possible by financial support from the Rapid Social Response (RSR) Program. RSR is a multidonor endeavor to help the world's poorest countries build effective social protection and labor systems that safeguard poor and vulnerable people against severe shocks and crises. RSR has been generously supported by Australia, Norway, the Russian Federation, Sweden, and the United Kingdom.

RAPID SOCIAL RESPONSE

Abbreviations

ADePT	Automated DEC Poverty Tables
cdf	cumulative distribution function
CGE	computable general equilibrium
CPI	consumer price index
FCU	foreign currency unit
GDP	gross domestic product
GIC	growth incidence curve
HIES	Household Income and Expenditure Survey
LAV	linkage aggregate variable
LCU	local currency unit
LFS	Labor Force Survey
MAMS	Maquette for MDG Simulations
MDG	Millennium Development Goals
NSO	National Statistics Office
PAL	Programa de Apoyo Alimentario
pdf	probability distribution function
UN	United Nations
WB	World Bank

Introduction

Predicting a macroeconomic shock—so that its impact can be addressed in advance—is difficult. Subsequent aftershocks can rapidly ripple through economies around the globe, often striking hardest those that can least tolerate the effects—developing countries and low-income subpopulations. Policy makers are challenged to design effective and timely policy responses that require insight into questions such as these:

- Which areas or regions are most likely to be affected, and in what way?
- How will the sectoral and regional impacts translate into impacts across the income or consumption distribution?
- What are the characteristics of those who will become poor as a result of the shock?
- What are the implications of the distribution of these impacts for the design of policy responses, particularly those responses that seek to provide safety nets to the affected?

To enable policy makers to formulate effective responses, these questions must be answered quickly. Because real-time data are often unavailable, particularly in developing countries, it would be advantageous to have a system that can explore solutions using data that predate the shock, rather than delay analysis until postshock data are collected.[1] Even when some real-time data are available from sectors or regions affected by a shock, exploring hypothetical scenarios using historical data can be useful in comparing alternative outcomes that may unfold in the future. In pursuit of these goals, the authors have developed a method and a software system that uses microdata to simulate outcomes of macroeconomic changes.

The traditional solution is to extrapolate poverty measures by estimating an "elasticity" of poverty to output. Although this approach is informative for the aggregate poverty impact, it provides limited guidance on what actions need to be taken. It cannot determine who is affected and to what extent. For instance, most targeted antipoverty programs are focused on the existing poor. However, when a macro shock occurs, any efforts to expand or retool these programs requires finding out who is likely to become poor and how much more deprivation is likely to occur among those who are already poor.

The ADePT Simulation Module, one of several modules in the ADePT platform,[2] offers a useful methodological framework for analysts interested in measuring how macroeconomic projections might affect households. The module's approach falls between simple extrapolation and the most sophisticated methods such as top-down or top-down-up models based on linking household data with computable general equilibrium (CGE) models. By using simple macroeconomic projections as the "macro-linkages" to a micro-behavioral model built from household data, the model captures the complexities that influence how macro impacts are transmitted to households. This approach offers time and cost advantages with only moderate data requirements.

The ADePT Simulation Module was originally developed to help analysts predict the distributional impact of macro shocks. However, it has much broader applications for macroeconomic analysis. It can be used, for example, to project outcomes of the economic status quo and to investigate the potential impact of structural reforms. The ADePT Simulation Module is an improvement over existing approaches because—with minimal data and computational requirements—it can evaluate in advance the distributional impacts of macroeconomic projections. By focusing on adjustments in employment and earnings, non-labor income, and price changes, it accounts for multiple transmission mechanisms and captures micro-level impacts across the entire income distribution. The method is leaner than the typical macro-micro model, computes rapidly, and works well in countries where CGE models are unavailable.

Additionally, the ADePT Simulation Module can be used to evaluate distributional measures, such as poverty and inequality, in the absence of real-time microdata. Most developing countries have collected microdata periodically in recent decades. This information has improved the monitoring of distributional indicators such as poverty and inequality indexes, among other objectives. However, economists still face the ongoing problem of how to update poverty and inequality measures over time. Additionally, there is the problem of how to estimate poverty and distributional impacts of macroeconomic projections based on structural reforms, expansion of social programs, or different macro shocks when real time microdata are absent.

Using existing macroeconomic data and household surveys, the ADePT Simulation Module helps in identifying and profiling those groups of individuals—defined by characteristics such as occupational sector, location, and education level—who are most likely to suffer income losses as a consequence of the change. This enables policy makers to both evaluate the effectiveness of existing safety nets and to design adequate responses when safety nets are lacking. It also provides information on possible "leading indicators" that can be monitored to rapidly gauge the likely welfare impacts of a shock in the absence of real-time information on household welfare.

The heterogeneity of individuals in household survey data enables the identification of those most likely to gain or lose as a result of a macroeconomic change. Results (simulated datasets) could, for example, profile the "new poor" or assess changes in unemployment resulting from the implementation of a particular policy. Other applications include exploring approaches for protecting the poorest from deprivation and evaluating the consequences of proposed policy measures.

As an example of the latter, the book examines in detail simulations for Poland and Mexico to evaluate the impact of increases in social assistance on poverty and income distribution. For each country, the ADePT Simulation Module was used to compute two scenarios. Results reveal the effectiveness of proposed policy decisions. The ability to quantitatively compare alternative outcomes simplifies the complex economic landscape and clarifies policy options.

Users need only limited knowledge of Stata or SPSS to prepare datasets for use in the ADePT Simulation Module, and they do not need to know how to program to undertake the complex analysis that ADePT performs. The ADePT Simulation Module produces three main types of outputs for crisis impact analysis:

1. It generates a new dataset that includes all the data provided in the baseline household survey plus information on simulated household and individual income (and consumption). Additionally, for individuals, it provides simulated labor force and corresponding employment status. These simulated data allow users to compare the characteristics of different groups of individuals and households (for example, households that become poor as a consequence of the macroeconomic shock versus those that do not). Users can also identify the characteristics of those most vulnerable to the simulated shock.

2. It produces and exports print-ready tables with a variety of data including the following:

   • Parameter estimates from the employment and earnings models used to simulate the impact of macroeconomic projections on the labor market
   • Income structure of households and its variation by component (labor and non-labor income) before and after projections
   • A summary of key statistics showing the performance of the simulation with respect to the inputs provided.

3. In combination with other ADePT modules, it produces and exports print-ready tables with information on the aggregate poverty and inequality impacts of the simulated macroeconomic projection.

Generated datasets can be used as inputs to other ADePT modules to perform additional analysis.

Analysts with backgrounds in statistics and econometrics will find this book to be a comprehensive resource for practical application of the ADePT Simulation Module. To ensure full understanding, all theoretical concepts are identified and explained. On completing this book, specialists will be able to analyze the impact of macroeconomic shocks and generate projections for hypothetical scenarios. These results will be helpful in informing governmental policy making. Students can use the module to replicate published results and develop their analytical skills.

This manual is organized in two parts. Part I covers the motivation, overview, and illustrations of the method. These chapters are strongly recommended because they provide a general view of the simulation process: how it operates, what kinds of questions this approach can answer, and how to interpret results, among other topics. It also presents a comprehensive description of the theoretical concepts behind each step of the microsimulation. In other words, it explains what the ADePT Simulation Module is doing behind the interface.

Part II describes each step the user must follow to create or obtain proper macro- and microeconomic inputs required for the simulation. It also explains how to enter these inputs into the module and the different options available for tailoring simulations. It provides guidelines for addressing the most common difficulties that may arise during the process, and discusses outputs produced by the module and how these can be used in additional analyses. Part II ends with a set of exercises and example solutions that mainly illustrate how different sections of the simulation process work independently of each other.

Notes

1. http://elibrary.worldbank.org/doi/book/10.1596/1813-9450-5705.
2. For information about installing ADePT software, see www.worldbank
   .org/adept.

PART I

Overview and Theoretical Concepts

Chapter 1

Motivations for the Methodology

Macroeconomic shocks are rarely predicted, making it difficult to create systems to deal with them in advance. Moreover, they often spread rapidly once they have begun, making their impacts difficult to track. As these shocks unravel and are transmitted throughout the global economy, they are likely to have large impacts on poverty, particularly in the developing world where employment is often more volatile and safety nets inadequate or nonexistent.

The distributional impact of such a shock is thus likely to be complex and dynamic. Given these complexities, a good analysis of these impacts must at least examine the following questions:

- Which sectors, areas, and regions are most likely to be affected, and in what way?
- How will the sector and regional impacts translate into impacts across the income or consumption distribution?
- What are the characteristics of those who will become poor as a result of the crisis?
- What implications does the distribution of these impacts have for the design of policy responses, particularly those responses that seek to provide safety nets to the affected?

To be useful to policy makers, these questions must be answered quickly. Because data are often not available on short notice, particularly in developing countries, it is imperative that a system be in place to generate answers beforehand. Such an approach would allow economists to work with available data that in most cases predate the shock rather than delay the analysis until such time as data become available, either during or after the shock. Even in countries where some real-time data *are* available from shock-affected sectors or regions, a prospective approach using historical data can be useful for simulating future impacts of hypothetical scenarios that are not available from real-time data—for example, to compare different alternative scenarios that may unfold in the future.

A tool for assessing poverty and distributional impacts of a rapidly changing shock must also be able to account for *multiple channels* through which the impacts can be transmitted to households and individuals. It must be able to identify the relative importance of these channels in a given country. It must also do so at the *individual and household levels* over the entire income or consumption distribution.

Although the ADePT Simulation Module can be used to analyze any macroeconomic projection, including most macro shocks, it was originally developed as a tool to examine the impacts of the global financial crisis. Like the macro shocks mentioned above, that crisis shifted rapidly, both across countries—via trade, financing, and remittances—and within countries—via adjustments in domestic credit and labor markets and fiscal policies. Although it began as a financial crisis in a few advanced economies, it quickly evolved into a job crisis in the developing world, with contractions in growth and large impacts on poverty (up to 120 million additional poor by some estimates). The crisis also had significant impacts on the distribution of income and consumption *among* the poor and non-poor, both within and between countries. As a result of these complex dynamics, the impacts of the crisis were extremely difficult to predict with a high degree of confidence, and a quick prospective approach was necessary to determine the impacts on distribution, so that policies could be devised to assist those most likely to be adversely affected by the crisis.

How the ADePT Simulation Module Compares with Other Approaches

Current approaches to prospectively analyzing the impact of a macroeconomic shock with the limited data available in most countries are inadequate in addressing the kinds of questions posed above. The most commonly and easily implemented methods used within the World Bank to assess the welfare (primarily consumption or income poverty) impacts of such shocks are the output-elasticity-of-poverty method and PovStat (World Bank PovertyNet).

The elasticity approach uses historical output and poverty trends to determine the responsiveness of poverty rates to growth in output (and consumption), which is then combined with macroeconomic projections to estimate the impacts of future reduced growth on poverty. Although this method is easy to implement and serves as a convenient benchmark, it is limited in its predictive capability because it yields only aggregate poverty impacts, with no account of the broader distributional effects. It may also prove deficient in predicting poverty impacts during a macroeconomic event that affects output growth in a way that is not entirely consistent with the recent growth experience in a country.

PovStat is an Excel-based World Bank simulation package. It uses household survey data and macroeconomic projections as inputs and estimates changes in poverty and inequality indicators. Although it allows for impacts to occur through multiple channels, it offers no easy way to account for changes in non-labor income (such as remittances). By focusing exclusively on household heads (and ignoring the employment status of other household members), PovStat also does not allow for a full accounting of labor market impacts. Perhaps the most significant limitation of PovStat is that it generates estimates for poverty and inequality (aggregated or disaggregated by regions or groups), but not the kind of distributional results that require individual or household-level projections.

More sophisticated simulation approaches have been used in some cases by the World Bank (Bourguignon, Bussolo, and Pereira da Silva 2008).[1] All are based on computable general equilibrium (CGE) or general equilibrium macroeconomic models that demand substantial information (for constructing social accounting matrices or time series of macroeconomic data) to create the "linkage aggregate variables" (LAVs) that are fed into the micro-simulation model. At the same time, most of these models do not allow for changes in some key features of the population, such as gender or age composition (Ferreira et al. 2008) with the exception of the Maquette for MDG [Millennium Development Goal] Simulations (MAMS). The main advantages of these models relate to improved accuracy of the counterfactual and consistency of the analysis. However, the information demands of these models make them difficult to apply in most developing countries, thus calling for an approach that is workable with available data and macroeconomic projections.

To improve on existing approaches—given the typical data constraints seen in most developing countries—the ADePT Simulation Module is able to evaluate the distributional impacts of a macroeconomic shock in advance with relatively few data and computational requirements. It allows the user to account for multiple transmission mechanisms and capture impacts at the micro level for the entire income distribution. The model allows this by focusing on labor market adjustments in employment and earnings, non-labor income, and price changes (with a view to the variation in food and non-food prices).

The particular microsimulation method underlying the ADePT Simulation Module is best seen as a compromise between the "aggregate" approaches and the complex macro-micro simulation approaches described above. The compromise involves combining the behavioral estimations from baseline household data with aggregated macroeconomic projections. This approach leads to a model that is leaner than the typical macro-micro simulation models, takes less time to compute, and above all, is applicable in countries where CGE models are either unavailable, outdated, or of poor quality. In contrast to CGE models, aggregate macroeconomic projections—such as those for national, sector, or regional GDP and remittances flows—are available for most countries with which the World Bank or the International Monetary Fund have an ongoing dialogue. Compared with the elasticity-based approach and PovStat, the ADePT Simulation Module has the advantage of being able to generate estimates for individuals and households all along the distribution with and without the change, which can be used for detailed poverty and distributional analyses of an impact.

Model Description and Simulation Methodology

Using microdata and macro projections, the ADePT Simulation Module can generate predictions for income distributions at the individual and house-hold levels for each year for which macroeconomic projections are available. The model superimposes macroeconomic projections on behavioral models built on microdata from before the onset of the shock. It is loosely based on the approaches described in Bourguignon Bussolo, and Pereira da Silva (2008) and Ferreira et al. (2008), with the important simplification of omitting the CGE component. Instead, the behavioral models are linked to aggregate and sector-level macroeconomic projections for a specific country and year, and the micro-level (individual and household) snapshot of future impacts is extrapolated from these projections.

The model focuses on labor markets and international remittances as the main channels through which the macro-level shocks are translated into impacts on individuals and households. It allows for shocks (negative or positive) to labor income—modeled as an employment shock, an earnings shock, or a combination of the two—and shocks to non-labor income, in the form of changes in remittances flows. Most of the changes in total income are captured this way, given that labor income and remittances account for a significant proportion of household income for most developing-country households. Reasonable assumptions are made about impacts on other sources of income, such as capital income, domestic remittances, rents, or public transfers.

The data requirements are fairly straightforward. At the macro level, information is needed on projected (1) changes, or growth rates, of output and employment by sector, and remittances; (2) population growth; and (3) price changes. At the micro level, a household survey is essential, with information on (1) household-level income or consumption (or both), (2) household and individual characteristics, and (3) individual-level labor force and employment status and earnings.

Outline of the Simulation Process

Macroeconomic projections of output (sector and national) are almost always available, but employment projections are usually not available. Thus, output growth estimates must be translated into employment changes at the sector level for a specific year and macroeconomic scenario. These estimates are typically made using sector output-employment elasticities (estimated from historical data), which are then applied to the output growth projections to generate changes in employment by sector.

Once the employment projections are generated, the three main steps in the simulation process are as illustrated in figure 1.1. The first step consists of using household data for the latest available baseline year to estimate behavioral models of employment status (whether an individual is employed, and the sector of employment) and earnings for individuals as a function of their individual and household characteristics.[2]

Figure 1.1: Diagram of the Modeling Process

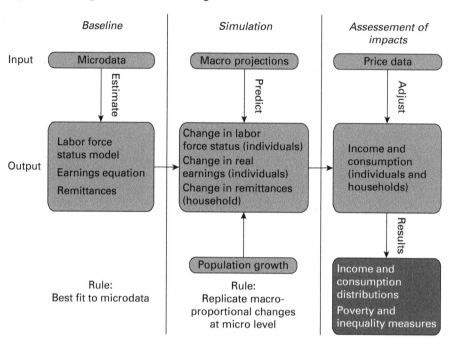

The second step consists of *replicating* the macro-level changes (projected changes in output and employment) between baseline and target years in the household data of the baseline year. This process uses the predictions of the behavioral models estimated on the baseline household data (as in step 1), and generates household- and individual-level predictions for employment, earnings, and remittances for specific target years and macroeconomic scenarios. Because an individual's labor income depends on employment status and labor earnings, how the output shock in a particular sector is apportioned between employment shocks, earnings shocks, and adjustments across sectors depends on how responsive (elastic) employment in that sector is to output changes. The output shock also implies that at the household level, the extent of the impact depends on the size of the aggregate shock at the sector level, and on the demographics and characteristics of household members, which determine their labor force status and earnings after the shock.

The simulations are also adjusted for population growth, using official population projections (disaggregated by gender and age group), to fully account for demographic changes that would affect the size and composition of the labor force and through that, the estimates of per capita household income. This adjustment is made by reweighting the households in the baseline data to replicate the demographic changes predicted by population projections.

To simulate changes in non-labor income, the projections of aggregate changes in remittances are linked to the baseline remittances information from household data using a simple assignment rule that ensures that the total change in remittances received by households is equal to the projected change in remittances from the macro data. Some components of non-labor income (profits, rents, and domestic remittances) are assumed to grow at the rate of aggregate GDP for the relevant period. Other components are kept constant in real terms at the preshock level or changed in accordance with specific information received for each country (social benefits, pensions, or other transfers, depending on the country).

The final step uses price projections to adjust the poverty line to reflect the difference in food and non-food inflation rates between baseline and target years. The absolute poverty line is typically anchored to a food basket that ensures a minimum calorie intake.[3] Thus, for countries where food inflation is expected to be significantly different from general inflation between baseline and projected years, the baseline poverty line would not be enough for a household to meet the basic food requirements in the projected year.[4]

Defining the "Impact" of a Macro Shock

The impact of the macro shock on poverty indices and income distribution can be measured in two ways:

- A "with-without" comparison, that is, the difference between with-shock and without-shock scenarios for the projected year (Type I impact)
- A "before-after" comparison, that is, the change in welfare status in a country between baseline and target years (Type II impact)

Each type of comparison can be useful in different cases, depending on the nature of the macroeconomic impact the country is likely to suffer from the macro shock and what the government us interested in knowing.

Figure 1.2: Type I and Type II Comparisons

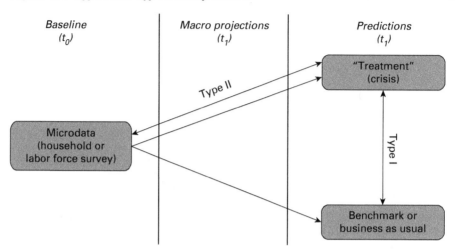

Figure 1.2 shows the difference in the definition of the impact of the shock for Type I and Type II comparisons. Because the definition of "impact" is different for the two types of comparisons, the results of the simulation should be read differently for the two types of comparisons as well.

It is important to note that the ADePT Simulation Module can also be used to examine the potential distributional impact of policy changes that can be measured through GDP growth or employment, such as changes in trade policies or structural reforms, among others. Moreover, it can be used to evaluate the relative effectiveness of various policy scenarios with differing aggregate impacts.[5]

Limitations and Assumptions

There are several caveats to using the ADePT Simulation Module. Some relate to issues relevant for microsimulation approaches in general, whereas others arise from the modifications adopted in its development. The main issues are the following:

- The quality of projections from the model depends on the nature and accuracy of the data underpinning the exercise. This issue is particularly important given the model's reliance on aggregate macroeconomic *projections*. Moreover, although macroeconomic projections are usually available for aggregated sectors like industry, services, and agriculture, the lack of availability of more disaggregated projections constrains the ability to account for heterogeneity *within* each sector.

- The simulation relies on behavioral models built on data that reflect the structure of labor markets and household incomes and their relationships with demographics as they stood *before* the shock. Consequently, the simulation assumes these structural relationships remain constant, not allowing for any changes over time or between scenarios. The more distant in the past the baseline year, the more questionable this assumption is likely to be.

- The model assumes that changes in labor market conditions are proportional to the projected change in outputs, based on the estimated past relationship between output and employment. This method implicitly assumes stable relationships between outputs, demand for labor, and labor earnings, which may not hold because of the distortions (such as segmentation and downward stickiness of nominal wages) that typically exist in the labor market and that are likely to affect adjustments during a shock.[6]

- The model does not allow for geographic mobility of factors (labor or capital) across time or scenarios. Thus, all individuals are assumed to remain at their place of origin, even if they experience a change in economic sector or employment status. This assumption is an abstraction from the truth, but it is likely to matter only when the results are disaggregated spatially or across rural and urban areas. The model does incorporate changes in domestic remittances from urban to rural areas—so the lack of factor mobility does not necessarily imply constant income flows across space.

- The model is limited in its ability to account for shifts in relative prices between different sectors of the economy resulting from the shock. Although the poverty impact of shifts in the price of food relative to other prices is taken into account, other potential sources of price impacts are ignored—for example, the general equilibrium effect of a change in the terms of trade between agriculture and other sectors. In the absence of a CGE model, it is nearly impossible to explicitly model for changes in terms of trade between sectors.

- To account for the channels through which output shocks are transmitted to households, the ADePT Simulation Module must predict individual and household-level incomes. But to provide poverty projections for a country that defines poverty according to *consumption,* household incomes must be converted into consumption using the questionable assumption that a household's propensity to consume is constant over time and across scenarios. In the absence of more information, however, this assumption at least has the advantage of being simple and transparent.

- The simulation component of the module relies on random draw using a pseudorandom number generator in computing the allocations of individuals into labor status, as well as labor market earnings of new workers and workers who are changing sectors. The module is configured such that the seed of this random number generator is the same over different runs, so generally the results will be reproducible. However, small changes in data may lead to changes in outcomes where the random components are required, and hence in the final figures. It should be understood that a part of the predicted change in distributional outcomes is due to these randomly simulated components.

Illustration and Interpretation of Typical Outputs

The ADePT Simulation Module helps identify typical results for impact analysis: aggregate poverty and inequality impacts, growth incidence curves, transition matrices, and a profile of those who are forced into poverty because of the macro shock (termed here the "new poor"). This section describes different types of results using simulated datasets conducted for the 2009 financial crisis in Bangladesh, Mexico, the Philippines, and Poland.

Poverty Impacts

Table 1.1 shows the aggregate poverty impacts of the financial crisis on Bangladesh, using baseline data from the 2005 Household Income and Expenditure Survey. The model generates a "business as usual" scenario and a "crisis" scenario. By examining the difference between the scenarios, the user can evaluate the aggregate poverty impact of the crisis. Note that this is a Type I impact, according to the terminology introduced earlier.

The table shows that for both moderate and extreme poverty lines, in general the reduction in incidence, gap, and severity of poverty would have been larger than had the crisis not occurred. That is, the welfare impact of

Table 1.1: Poverty Impacts of the Financial Crisis in Bangladesh – Type I

	Baseline	Business as usual		Crisis		Impact	
	2005	2009	2010	2009	2010	2009	2010
Moderate poverty							
Headcount rate (%)	40.0	28.2	24.6	28.6	25.8	0.4	1.2
Poverty gap (%)	9.0	5.9	5.0	6.0	5.3	0.1	0.3
Severity of poverty (%)	2.9	1.8	1.5	1.9	1.6	0.1	0.1
Extreme poverty							
Headcount rate (%)	25.1	16.5	13.9	16.7	14.8	0.2	0.9
Poverty gap (%)	4.7	2.9	2.4	3.0	2.5	0.1	0.1
Severity of poverty (%)	1.3	0.8	0.6	0.8	0.7	0	0.1
Inequality (per capita expenditure)							
Gini coefficient	0.310	0.321	0.324	0.341	0.320	0.020	–0.004
Theil index	0.186	0.197	0.199	0.222	0.194	0.025	–0.005

Source: Habib et al. 2010a.

the crisis worked against the status quo trend of improvement in welfare. Inequality indicators, however, were largely unaffected, likely because subtle changes in the income distribution (which could greatly affect some groups) remain undetected by these aggregate indicators. These changes can be detected by other outputs, as shown below.

Table 1.2 shows the same results for Mexico, except that the comparison is made between a "precrisis" (2008) scenario and a "crisis" (2010) scenario. Thus, the impact gleaned from this table is a Type II impact. The initial impact in 2009 is large by all poverty measures, but the headcount poverty rate is lowered each year thereafter as the crisis subsides. Again, inequality indicators remain unaffected. This comparison is useful because it demonstrates how the ADePT Simulation Module is able to capture the differences in the timing and nature of the crisis impacts across the two countries.

Growth Incidence Curves

To get a better sense of the more nuanced distributional impacts of a shock, growth incidence curves (GICs) can be generated to examine how income losses are allocated across households. For this purpose, the module maps out income losses between the "baseline" (or "precrisis") and "crisis" scenarios at every percentile in both the urban and rural income distributions. It orders households according to their precrisis per capita household income level (from lowest to highest), groups them into income percentiles (as defined in the baseline case), and plots the average percentage loss in per capita

Table 1.2: Poverty Impacts of the Financial Crisis in Mexico – Type II

	Baseline	Projected		
	2008	2009	2010	2011
Moderate poverty				
Headcount rate (%)	47.5	50.9	49.9	48.8
Poverty gap (%)	20.3	22.4	21.9	21.2
Severity of poverty (%)	12.0	13.6	13.2	12.6
Extreme poverty				
Headcount rate (%)	19.1	21.6	21.1	20.2
Poverty gap (%)	8.0	9.3	9.0	8.5
Severity of poverty (%)	5.1	6.0	5.9	5.4
Inequality (per capita income)				
Gini coefficient	0.52	0.52	0.52	0.52
Theil index	0.64	0.66	0.66	0.66

Source: World Bank 2010.

household income by percentile. This exercise is performed for all households, as well as for specific groups. Each GIC constructed in this manner allows the user to compare percentage income losses across households within the group.

Figure 1.3 is an example of a GIC for the Philippines, and shows some important differences between urban and rural areas. The urban GIC shows greater impacts for the bottom 10 percent of the distribution and weaker impacts above the seventieth percentile, while the rural GIC is quite flat, with marginally greater impacts seen only for some of the poorest (below the tenth percentile) and wealthier (seventieth to ninetieth percentile) groups. It is important to note that the expenditure percentiles are defined with reference to each area (urban or rural). Because urban areas are better off, on average, than rural areas, the kth percentile of urban households is better off than (and thus not strictly comparable with) the kth percentile of rural households.[7]

Transition Matrices

GICs provide information about income gains or losses incurred by the average household within each percentile of the income distribution, and are thus useful in identifying which income groups suffer relatively larger or smaller changes. However, GICs can hide a significant amount of heterogeneity in the absolute size of impacts, even among households with very similar baseline or initial per capita household income levels.

An alternative is to examine the size of the income shock suffered by households in each income group. This examination uses matrices constructed by deciles of per capita income, keeping the upper and lower limits of each decile fixed at the initial income levels. Figure 1.4 shows an example of a transition matrix for Poland, and plots the share

Figure 1.3: Growth Incidence Curve for The Philippines

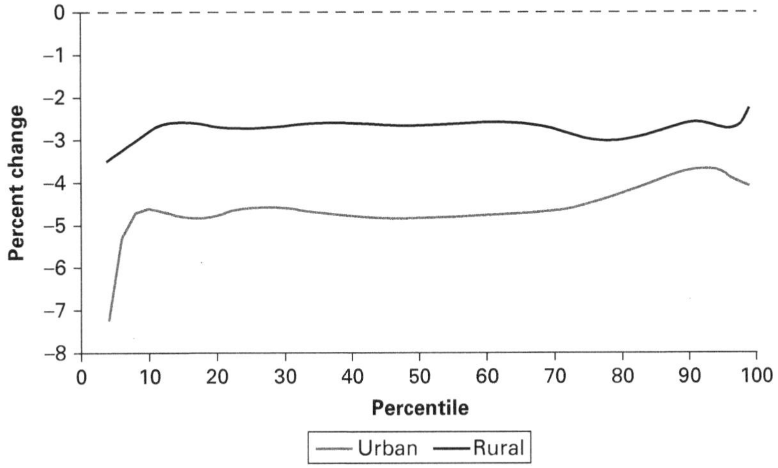

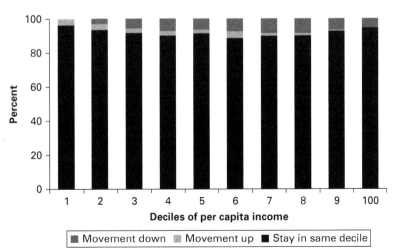

Source: Habib et al. 2010b.

Figure 1.4: Transitions across Deciles of per Capita Income – Poland

Source: Habib et al. 2012.

15

of households in each decile that (1) suffer an income loss large enough to shift them to a lower income decile or more, (2) suffer a relatively small income movement and therefore their position remains unchanged, and (3) experience a positive change and are better off in the projected year.

Those households in the middle of the distribution are the hardest hit as measured by the absolute level of income change. Although most households tend to stay in the same decile, approximately 10 percent of all households suffer income losses that push them to a lower decile. Even movements upward are generally rare in many countries. Poland shows some upward movement as a result of safety nets (particularly unemployment insurance) that protect households at the bottom of the distribution and move them up to a different decile.

Profiling the "New Poor"[8]

Finally, the ADePT Simulation Module offers a means for determining which groups are most likely to be forced into poverty as a result of a macroeconomic shock (but who were not poor before the onset of the shock). In general, these households are likely to suffer large income losses that drive them below the poverty line. By determining a profile of these households, the user can identify links between income losses and certain characteristics that the households may have in common. With this knowledge, policy makers can devise policies to specifically target these vulnerable groups.

Figure 1.5 and 1.6 show examples of such an analysis from three different applications of the microsimulation model. The figures show that the "new poor" households are more likely to live in urban areas with more educated household heads than structurally poor households but less likely than the average household. For instance, the pattern with regard to the urban-rural breakdown was more pronounced in the Philippines. Figure 1.5 shows that 57 percent of the Filipino new poor households lived in rural areas (close to the national average of 51 percent) compared with 74 percent of structurally poor households.

Figure 1.6 shows that the characteristics of "new poor" household heads are also significantly different from those of other groups in the population. In all three countries, "new poor" household heads are relatively more skilled than those of structurally poor households, but less skilled than those

Figure 1.5: Percentage of Households in Rural Areas

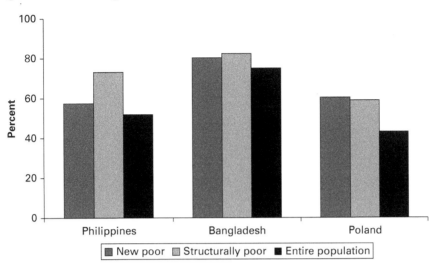

Source: Habib et al. 2012.

Figure 1.6: Percentage of Households that Have Low-Skilled Heads

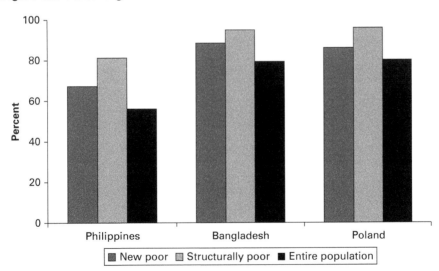

Source: Habib et al. 2012.

17

of the average household. This skill level is consistent with the pattern of middle-income households suffering the largest impacts (in absolute terms) from the crisis, given that they are more likely to be urban and employed in the formal sector (and therefore more skilled) than household heads among the structurally poor.

Notes

1. These include the micro-accounting approach (computable general equilibrium [CGE]–representative household groups), top-down micro simulations models (CGE–micro or macro models), and feedback loops from bottom to top (Bourguignon, Bussolo, and Pereira da Silva 2008).
2. Employment status (through a multinomial model) is estimated separately for low and high skill levels, and earnings (an ordinary least squares model) are estimated separately for each sector.
3. This refers to a poverty line defined over the consumption space.
4. Note that by construction, the projected income or consumption distribution for a crisis year is expressed using prices in the baseline year, which implies that to obtain poverty estimates that are comparable with the baseline estimates, the baseline poverty line should be kept unchanged in real terms.
5. The ADePT Simulation Module cannot be classified among the fiscal microsimulation models.
6. Sectoral movements of labor are modeled as depending on individual and household characteristics (through the multinomial logit model) and population growth. This approach may not fully capture the kinds of structural shifts that have apparently been observed in some countries following the global financial crisis, such as a reduction in the relative demand for skilled labor.
7. Because the extreme bounds of the distribution are particularly noisy, the distribution was trimmed at the lowest and highest percentiles to make the graph more readable.
8. See Habib et al. 2012.

References

Bourguignon, F., M. Bussolo, and L. Pereira da Silva. 2008. "The Impact of Macroeconomic Policies on Poverty and Income Distribution: Macro-Micro Evaluation Techniques and Tools." In *The Impact of Macroeconomic Policies on Poverty and Income Distribution: Macro-Micro Evaluation Techniques and Tools*, edited by F. Bourguignon, M. Bussolo, and L. Pereira da Silva. Washington, DC: World Bank.

Ferreira, F., P. Leite, L. Pereira da Silva, and P. Picchetti. 2008. "Can the Distributional Impacts of Macroeconomic Shocks Be Predicted? A Comparison of Top-Down Macro-Micro Models with Historical Data for Brazil." In *The Impact of Macroeconomic Policies on Poverty and Income Distribution: Macro-Micro Evaluation Techniques and Tools*, edited by F. Bourguignon, M. Bussolo, and L. Pereira da Silva. Washington, DC: World Bank.

Habib, B., A. Narayan, S. Olivieri, and C. Sánchez-Páramo. 2010a. "Assessing Ex Ante the Poverty and Distributional Impact of the Global Crisis in a Developing Country: A Micro-simulation Approach with Application to Bangladesh." Policy Research Working Paper 5238, World Bank, Washington, DC.

———. 2010b. "Assessing Ex Ante the Poverty and Distributional Impact of the Global Crisis in The Philippines: A Micro-simulation Approach." Policy Research Working Paper 5286, World Bank, Washington, DC.

———. 2012. "Assessing the Poverty and Distributional Impacts of the Financial Crisis with Microsimulations: An Overview of Country Studies." In *Knowing, When You Do Not Know: Simulating the Poverty and Distributional Impacts of an Economic Crisis*, edited by A. Narayan and C. Sánchez-Páramo. Washington, DC: World Bank.

World Bank. 2010. "Recent Trends and Forecasts of Poverty in Mexico: A Poverty Note." Unpublished, Latin America and the Caribbean Region, World Bank, Washington, DC.

Chapter 2

Technical Discussion

This chapter provides technical details about the economic model and describes the steps involved in using the ADePT Simulation Module. The chapter is organized in three main sections: baseline, simulation, and assessment.

Baseline

This first step is the process by which individual and household-level information is used to estimate a set of parameters and unobserved characteristics for various equations of the household income–generation model. This section first presents a brief description of the model, then describes the econometric strategy used for the behavioral model of employment status and earning equations.

The Model

The model behind the ADePT Simulation Module is the household income–generation model developed by Bourguignon and Ferreira (2005). This model allows accounting for multiple transmission channels and operating at the individual and household levels. The first component of the model is an identity that defines the per capita income in a household h

as the ratio between the total household income and the total number of members (n_h) in that household:

$$y_h = \frac{1}{n_h}\left[\sum_{i=1}^{n_h}\sum_{L=1}^{\Lambda}\sum_{j=0}^{J}I_{hi}^{Lj}\,y_{hi}^{Lj} + y_{0h}\right],\tag{2.1}$$

in which i = household member

$\qquad L$ = level of education

$\qquad \Lambda$ = maximum level of education of the individual

$\qquad j$ = labor status

$\qquad J$ = economic sector

$\qquad I_{hi}^{Lj}$ is an indicator function of labor status j of individual i with level of education L

$\qquad y_{hi}^{Lj}$ = earnings of individual i with level of education L in economic sector j

$\qquad y_{0h}$ = total non-labor income received by household h

The total household income—the expression in brackets in equation (2.1)—results from adding two main sources of family income: *labor* and *non-labor* income. At the same time, total family labor income is the aggregation of earnings in different economic sectors across members.[1] So, the equation shows not only whether an individual participates (or does not participate) in the sector, but also whether that individual receives (or does not receive) wages for that job. The labor participation model relies on the utility maximization approach developed by McFadden (1974). Assume that the utility (U_{hi}^{Lj}) for individual i of household h, associated with labor status $j = 0,\ldots, J$, and level of education L, can be expressed as a linear function of observed individual and household characteristics (Z_{hi}^{L}) and unobserved utility determinants of the occupational status (v_{i}^{Lj}) (equation (2.2)). Furthermore, individual i chooses sector j (the indicator function $I_{hi}^{Lj} = 1$; equation (2.3)) if economic sector j provides the highest level of utility[2]:

$$U_{hi}^{Lj} = Z_{hi}^{L}\psi^{Lj} + v_{i}^{Lj}\tag{2.2}$$

$$I_{hi}^{Lj} = 1 \; if \; U_{hi}^{Lj} \geq U_{hi}^{Ll}\tag{2.3}$$

with $j = 0, \ldots, J$ and L = education level
for all $l = 0, \ldots, J, \forall l \neq j$

Each individual must choose from five or six alternatives: being inactive, unemployed, or being in an economic sector (for example, agriculture, manufacturing, other industries, or services). The criterion value associated with being inactive is arbitrarily set to zero. The unobserved utility determinants of each occupation status are assumed to be identically and independently distributed across individuals, occupations, and skill levels.

The observed heterogeneity in earnings in each economic sector j can be modeled by a log-linear function of observed individual and household characteristics (X_{hi}^L) and unobserved factors (μ_{hi}^{Lj}) as a standard Mincer equation (Mincer 1974). These earnings functions are defined independently on each economic sector by skill level (L):

$$\log y_{hi}^{Lj} = X_{hi}^L \Omega^{Lj} + \mu_{hi}^{Lj} \; for \; i = 1,\ldots,n_h \; and \; j = 1,\ldots,J. \qquad (2.4)$$

The second component of total household income, total family *non-labor* income, is the sum of different elements at the household level such as international (η_h^I) and domestic remittances (η_h^D); rents, interest, and dividends on capital (k_h); social transfers (tr_h); and other sources of non-labor income (z_h), as in equation (2.5):

$$y_{0h} = \eta_h^I + \eta_h^D + k_h + tr_h + z_h. \qquad (2.5)$$

The analysis focuses only on international remittances and makes some minimal assumptions about other components. Ideally, international remittances would be modeled, but migration-related information in most surveys is poor or insufficient. A simple nonparametric assignment rule that is consistent with the existing evidence is better.

Equations (2.1) to (2.5) complete the model. Total household income is a nonlinear function of the observed characteristics of the household and its members and the unobserved characteristics of household members. This function depends on a set of parameters: those of the occupational-choice model for each skill level and those in the earnings functions for each economic sector and skill level. The model assumes that there is no variation in the composition of the household. In other words, the number, age, and gender of members of a household remain constant over time. Demographic change is incorporated through calibration of the survey weights.

Estimation Strategy for the Baseline

The model's baseline requires some econometric estimation work for both the occupational choice model and earnings model. This work is necessary to provide an initial set of coefficients (ψ^{Lj}, Ω^{Lj}) as well as an estimate of the unobserved characteristics (v_i^{Lj}, μ_{hi}^{Lj}), respectively, for the occupational choice model and the earnings equations. These estimations are based on individual working-age population data (between 15 and 64 years old). These equations (2.3 and 2.4) should be estimated simultaneously because of the likely correlation among the unobservable terms in the labor-supply decision and earnings model. The ADePT Simulation Module supports the Bourguignon, Fournier, and Gurgand (2007) correction method that includes the following bias correction terms, akin to the inverse Mills' ratios in the Heckman model (Wooldridge 2002): $\lambda_j = m(P_j)$ for the chosen alternative j, and $\lambda_j = \dfrac{P_j m(P_j)}{P_j - 1}$ for the alternatives not chosen, in which

$$m(P) = \int_{-\infty}^{+\infty} \Phi^{-1}\big(G(v - \ln P)\big)\varphi(v)\,dv, \quad \varphi(z)$$ is the standard normal probability

density function (pdf), $\Phi(z)$ is the standard normal cumulative distribution function (cdf), and $G(u)$ is the cdf of the extreme value distribution.

Occupational Choice Model

The parameters of the occupational choice model can be obtained using a multinomial logit model under the assumption that the unobservable (v_i^{Lj}) are identically and independently distributed across choices and individuals and have a double exponential distribution (Type 1 extreme value distribution) with pdf and cdf given by equations (2.6) and (2.7):

$$f\left(v_i^{Lj}\right) = \exp\left[-\exp\left(-v_i^{Lj}\right)\right]\exp(-v_i^{Lj}) \tag{2.6}$$

$$F\left(v_i^{Lj}\right) = \exp\left[-\exp\left(-v_i^{Lj}\right)\right]. \tag{2.7}$$

The estimation of the parameters of interest is conducted on all working-age individuals, separately for low and high skill levels. The labor force and employment decisions within the household are modeled only by inclusion of the household head binary variable and its interactions with gender and marital status. The set of explanatory variables includes not only an individual's sociodemographic characteristics (age, gender, maximum education level, if head of household, and so on) but also the household's characteristics, such as size, dependency ratio, and geographic area, among others.

So, the parameters as well as the probability of being in each state can be estimated at the individual level (equation (2.8)), considering zero as the reference category (inactivity):

$$P_{hi}^{Lj} = \frac{exp\left[Z_{hi}^{Lj}\left(\psi^{Lj} - \psi^{L0}\right)\right]}{1 + \sum_{j=1}^{J} exp\left[Z_{hi}^{Lj}\left(\psi^{Lj} - \psi^{L0}\right)\right]} \quad for \ j = 1,\dots,J \qquad (2.8)$$

$$P_{hi}^{L0} = 1 - \sum_{j=1}^{J} P_{hi}^{Lj}. \qquad (2.9)$$

To estimate the individual utility level of being in each labor state, values for the residual terms were drawn randomly in a way that is consistent with observed occupational choices. Train and Wilson (2008) define the distribution functions of the extreme value errors conditional on the chosen alternative. Assume alternative zero is chosen ($j = 0$) and denote $Z_{hi}^L \widehat{\psi}^{Lj} = V_{hi}^{Lj}$ for $j = 0 \dots, j.$[3] Define $\widehat{V}_{hi}^{0j} = V_{hi}^0 - V_{hi}^j$ and $D_{hi}^0 = \sum_{j=0}^{j} exp\left(-\widehat{V}_{hi}^{0j}\right),$ in which $P_{hi}^0 = 1/D_{hi}^0$ is the logit choice probability. Then the cdf for the alternative chosen v_{hi}^0 is given by equation 2.10:

$$F(v_{hi}^0 \mid alternative \ 0 \ is \ chosen) = exp\left(-D_{hi}^0 exp\left(v_{hi}^0\right)\right). \qquad (2.10)$$

Calculating the inverse of this distribution yields equation (2.11):

$$\widehat{v}_{hi}^0 = \ln\left(D_{hi}^0\right) - \ln\left(-\ln\left(\mu\right)\right), \qquad (2.11)$$

in which μ is a draw from a uniform distribution between 0 and 1. Error terms for other alternatives $\left(v_{hi}^j \ with \ j \neq 0\right)$ must be calculated conditioned on the error terms of the alternative chosen $(\widehat{v}_{hi}^0)$. The distribution for these errors is given by equation (2.12):

$$F(v_{hi}^j \mid alternative \ 0 \ is \ chosen, j \geq 1) = \frac{exp\left(-exp\left(-v_{hi}^j\right)\right)}{exp\left(-exp\left(-\left(\widehat{V}_{hi}^{0j} + \widehat{v}_{hi}^0\right)\right)\right)} \qquad (2.12)$$

$$for \ v_{hi}^j < \left(\widehat{V}_{hi}^{0j} + v_{hi}^0\right).$$

The inverse of this distribution is given by equation (2.13):

$$\hat{v}_{hi}^{j} = -\ln\left(-\ln\left(m\left(\hat{v}_{hi}^{0}\right)\mu\right)\right), \tag{2.13}$$

$$where\ m\left(\hat{v}_{hi}^{0}\right) = \exp(-\exp\left(-\left(\widehat{V}_{hi}^{0j} + \hat{v}_{hi}^{0}\right)\right),$$

in which μ is a draw from a uniform distribution between 0 and 1. Repeating this same method when an alternative other than zero is chosen and using expressions (2.9) to (2.13), individual utility levels for each alternative can be calculated according to equation (2.14):

$$\widehat{U}_{hi}^{Lj} = Z_{hi}^{Lj}\widehat{\psi}_{hi}^{Lj} + \hat{v}_{hi}^{Lj}\ for\ j \geq 0. \tag{2.14}$$

Earnings Equations

The coefficients of earnings functions for each sector and skill level are obtained by ordinary least squares estimation. The process assumes homoskedastic normal distributions for residual terms, and is given formally by equation (2.15):

$$\hat{y}_{hi}^{Lj} = \exp\left(X_{hi}\widehat{\Omega}^{Lj} + \hat{\varepsilon}_{hi}^{Lj}\right)\ for\ i = 1,\dots,n_h \tag{2.15}$$

$$\hat{\varepsilon}_{hi}^{Lj} \sim N\left(0, \hat{\sigma}^{2}\right).$$

Simulation

The second step, simulation, consists of replicating macroeconomic simulated changes (that is, sector employment, total output, or remittances) between the baseline and projected years on changes in different components of the household income–generation model (that is, labor and non-labor income). This process is divided into three sub-steps ordered in the following sequence: population growth, labor market status and income, and non-labor income.

Population Growth

The population growth adjustment is particularly important in countries with high fertility rates or significant immigration flows, or when the last available household survey is relatively far from the projected year. In the first case, the number of labor market entrants rises faster than overall population. In practical terms, the adjustment for population growth allows the analysis to explicitly take into account changes in the size of the working-age population, and hence to distinguish between employment growth driven (or rather absorbed) by demographic trends and net (or additional) employment growth.

In most household surveys, the household is the unit that is sampled, thus, the probability of including an individual conditional on the household being selected is 1.[4] In other words, the survey weights attached to every individual within the household should be equal. In this sense the initial or prior weights can be written as in equation (2.16):

$$\sum_h \sum_i w_{hi} = N, \tag{2.16}$$

in which N is the initial total population and
$$w_{hi} = w_{hj} = w_h \quad for\ i \neq j \wedge i, j \in h.$$

The variable w_{hi} is the weight of individual i within household h, equal to the common weight w_h. So, equation (2.16) can be rewritten as equation (2.17):

$$\sum_h w_h\ household\ size = \sum_h w_h^* = N. \tag{2.17}$$

Equation (2.17) can be written in terms of probabilities:

$$1 = \sum_h \frac{w_h^*}{N} = \sum_h q_h^*. \tag{2.18}$$

Given a new structure or total population to estimate:

$$\sum_h \sum_i \tilde{w}_{hi}\ 1\ \left[age\ group, gender\right] = \tilde{N}\left[age\ group, gender\right] \tag{2.19}$$

$$\sum_h \sum_i \tilde{w}_{hi} = \tilde{N}, \tag{2.20}$$

in which 1 [age group, gender] is the indicator function, $\tilde{N}$ is the new total population, and each member i of household h has the same weight,

$$\tilde{w}_{hi} = \tilde{w}_{hj} = \tilde{w}_h \quad for\ i \neq j \wedge i, j \in h\ then$$
$$\sum_h \tilde{w}_h\ household\ size = \sum_h \hat{w}_h = \tilde{N}. \tag{2.21}$$

Equation (2.22) expresses this in probability terms:

$$1 = \sum_h \frac{\hat{w}_h}{\tilde{N}} = \sum_h \hat{r}_h.$$

(2.22)

The idea is to go from the initial weight (w_h^*) or probability (q_h^*) distribution to a new one $(\hat{w}_h$ or $\hat{r}_h)$ imposing several constraints such as gender or age-group population growth rates. Formally, the new probability distribution can be obtained by solving the optimization problem in equation (2.23)

$$\min I(r, q) = \sum_h r_h^* \ln\left(\frac{r_h^*}{q_h^*}\right),$$

(2.23)

such that

$$E(x_g) = \sum_h r_h^* \, m_{x_g h} \quad g = 1,...,G$$

(2.24)

$$\sum_h r_h^* = 1.$$

The term $m_{x_g h}$ is the mean of the x_g characteristic within the household

$$h \left(m_{x_g h} = \frac{\sum_i x_{gih}}{hhsize_h} \right).$$ In other words, this optimization procedure asserts that the distribution r_h^* that meets the moment constraints and the normalization restriction while requiring the least additional information should be picked, and the one that deviates as little as possible from the initial distribution (q_h^*) should be picked. The solution to this problem is given by equation (2.25):

$$\hat{r}_h = q_h^* \frac{\exp\left(X\hat{\lambda}\right)}{\Omega\left(\hat{\lambda}\right)} \rightarrow \sum_h \hat{w}_h = \sum_h w_h^* \theta_h = \tilde{N} \text{ with } \theta_h = \frac{\exp\left(X\tilde{\lambda}\right)}{\Omega\left(\tilde{\lambda}\right)},$$

(2.25)

in which $\hat{\lambda}$ is the Lagrange multiplier for the constraint $E(X)$, and Ω is the normalizing factor to scale the new population to the target size. In the simulation process the analysis imposes several population constraints that result from different growth rates by gender and age-group brackets.

Labor Income

One of the transmission channels that the model focuses on is labor markets. This transmission channel is modeled not only from the employment structure side but also from the earnings side of the economy. In this sense, it allows for shocks (negative or positive) to labor income as an employment shock, an earnings shock, or a combination. This section is divided into three sub-steps in the following sequence: labor status allocation, labor income imputation, and matching total economic growth.

Labor Status Allocation: Out of or In Labor Force, Unemployment, and Economic Sector of Employment

This first sub-step consists of reassigning working-age individuals between employment statuses and across economic sectors to match the projected aggregate changes in total employment and in economic sectors. The reallocation method, as Bourguignon, Robilliard, and Robinson (2005) point out, assumes *neutrality* of changes with respect to individual or household characteristics. In other words, the labor status changes are restricted to changes in the *intercepts* of the occupational criterion function. The relative change in the ex ante utility that an individual has depends only on the initial ex ante utility of the various occupational choices rather than on individual or household characteristics.

The steps require the following inputs:

- Estimated utility from the baseline (see the "Occupational Choice Model" section): $\widehat{U}_{hi}^{j} = \widehat{\psi}_{0}^{j} + Z_{hi}\widehat{\psi}^{j} + \hat{v}_{i}^{j}$, with $j = 0, \ldots, J$
- New population shares in each status, which represents the target vector: $\hat{p}^{j}$, with $j = 0, \ldots, J$
- New population structure weights (see the "Population Growth" section): $\hat{w}_{hi}$
- Fixed base outcome as in the multinomial logit model, that is, inactivity

The method follows an iterative procedure of adjusting the intercepts of the multinomial logit with additive constants (γ^{j}, with $j = 0, \ldots, J$) to achieve the target allocations. The procedure is initiated by setting all additive constants to the relative change according to macro projections using inactivity as the reference category. Thus, the inactivity additive constant is set to zero for identification purposes: $\gamma^{0} = 0$. Then the algorithm follows the sequence of steps described here:

1. Compute the new utility based on the new intercept:
$$\tilde{U}_{hi}^{j} = \psi_{0}^{j*} + Z_{hi}\widehat{\psi}^{j} + \hat{v}_{i}^{j}, \text{with } \psi_{0}^{j*} = \widehat{\psi}_{0}^{j} + \gamma^{j}$$

(2.26)

   for $j = 0, \ldots, J$ and $\gamma^{0} = 0$.

2. Select the labor status with the greatest utility by individual:
$\breve{U}_{hi}^{j} = \text{argmax}_{j=0,...,J}\left(\tilde{U}_{hi}^{j}\right)$.

3. Calculate the weighted totals ($\tilde{T}^{j}$) in each labor status:

$$\tilde{T}^{j} = \sum_{i}\hat{w}_{hi}^{j}\, 1\left[\breve{U}_{hi}^{j} = j\right] \tag{2.27}$$

$$\tilde{p}^{j} = \frac{\tilde{T}^{j}}{\sum_{i}\hat{w}_{hi}}, \forall j = 0,...,J. \tag{2.28}$$

4. Vary parameters $\psi_{0}^{j^{*}}, \forall j = 0,...,J$, and repeat the procedure described in steps 1–3 until a minimum of a Pearson χ^{2} quadratic loss is found:

$$P\left(\psi^{*}\right) = \sum_{j=0}^{J}\frac{(\tilde{p}^{j} - \hat{p}^{j})^{2}}{\hat{p}^{j}}. \tag{2.29}$$

Labor Income Imputation

The second sub-step consists of assigning a labor income to each individual of the working-age population sample (or taking the income away) according to the individual's "new" labor status. There are three possible cases: the first one sets positive labor income to zero for those individuals who were employed in the baseline and become unemployed or inactive as a consequence of the macro projection. In the second case, the previous labor income (y_{hi}^{j}) is assigned when individuals remain employed in the same economic sector as in the baseline. In the third case, the earnings model estimated as part of the baseline is used to predict earnings ($\hat{y}_{hi}^{j}$) for two groups of workers: those with no previous earning history (that is, those who come from inactivity or unemployment) and those who change employment sector. Formally, the "new" vector of earnings for the working-age population will be defined as in equation (2.30):

$$\tilde{y}_{hi}^{j} = \begin{cases} 0 \text{ when } \hat{U}_{hj}^{j} \neq \breve{U}_{hi}^{s} \text{ for } j > 1 \text{ and } s = 0 \text{ or } 1 \\ y_{hi}^{j} \text{ when } \hat{U}_{hi}^{j} = \breve{U}_{hi}^{s} \text{ for } j = s > 1 \qquad \forall i \in [15, 64 \text{ years old}] \\ \hat{y}_{hi}^{j} \text{ when } \hat{U}_{hi}^{j} \neq \breve{U}_{hi}^{s} \text{ for } j = 0 \text{ or } 1 \text{ and } s > 1. \end{cases}$$

$$\tag{2.30}$$

Note that all workers who do not belong to the working-age population sample are assumed to remain in their baseline employment status as well as receive their baseline labor earnings.

Matching the Total Growth

Sector Growth

Once all workers have been assigned positive labor earnings, total earnings in a sector are adjusted to match aggregate projected changes in output. The third sub-step relies on the fact that projected changes in sector output can be explained by projected changes in sector employment and projected changes in sector earnings and profits, and assumes that earnings and profits grow at the same rate.

The treatment of public sector workers and those with more than one job differs slightly from what was just described. Total public sector employment is assumed to remain constant (no individuals are assigned in or out of the public sector) and labor earnings of public sector workers are adjusted in line with their sector mapping (that is, into agriculture, industry, or services).[5] Similarly, for those holding more than one job, the model assumes the sector of employment of their secondary activity remains constant while earnings are adjusted in line with sector change.

The sector adjustment can be divided into three steps. The first step computes the total target income by economic sector (Y_1^{jT}) as the product of the total sector income from the microdata at the baseline year (Y_0^{jT}) and the sector growth rate between the initial and projected year from the macro projections by sector (δ_{GDP}^j). Formally, see equation (2.31):

$$Y_1^{jT} = Y_0^{jT}\left(1+\delta_{GDP}^j\right), \ \forall j = 2,\ldots,J. \qquad (2.31)$$

The total sector income is the weighted sum of all labor earnings in main and secondary occupations in the initial year of all working population employed in that particular sector (i.e., manufacturing, agriculture, industry, services) (equation (2.32)):

$$Y_0^{jT} = \sum_i \left(y_{hi}^{jp}\, w_{hi}\mathbb{1}\left[\widehat{U}_{hi}^j = j\right] + y_{hi}^{js}\, w_{hi}\mathbb{1}\left[I_{hi}^{js} = j\right]\right), \ \forall j = 2,\ldots,J. \quad (2.32)$$

The second step (equation (2.33)) calculates the "new" total income, considering not only the adjustments already made through the labor market (employment structure and earnings), but also through population growth.

$$\hat{Y}_1^{jT} = \sum_i \left(\tilde{y}_{hi}^{jp} \ \hat{w}_{hi} \mathbb{1}\left[\breve{U}_{hi}^j = j \right] + y_{hi}^{js} \ \hat{w}_{hi} \mathbb{1}\left[I_{hi}^{js} = j \right] \right), \forall j = 2, \dots, J. \quad (2.33)$$

The third step rescales the "new" total income (equation (2.33)) up to the point where it meets the total income target (equation (2.31)) for each economic sector, as shown in equation (2.34):

$$\hat{Y}_1^{jT} = Y_1^{jT}, \ \forall j = 2, \dots, J. \quad (2.34)$$

Total Growth

So far, the simulation replicates the macro growth rate by economic sector. However, the growth rate for the total economy based on the microdata is, generally, different from that reported by macro projections. The reason for this disparity is explained by unequal economic sector structures in the micro and macro data. We prioritize the match of growth rates for the total economy between macro- and microdata over the match of growth rates for economic sectors. To do that prioritization, first, all labor incomes by economic sectors are rescaled, keeping constant the total volume of the economy. The result is then shifted by the growth rate of total GDP.

Components of Non-Labor Income

Non-labor income is the sum of different income elements at the household level such as international (η_h^I) and domestic remittances (η_h^D); rents, interest, and dividends on capital (k_h); social transfers (tr_h); and other forms of non-labor income (z_h) (equation (2.35)).

$$y_{0h} = \eta_h^I + \eta_h^D + k_h + tr_h + z_h, \forall h. \quad (2.35)$$

The model focuses only on international remittances and makes some minimal assumptions about other components.

International Remittances

Ideally, international remittances would be modeled, but migration-related information in most surveys is poor or insufficient. A simple nonparametric assignment rule that is consistent with the existing evidence is better.

The method is divided into two main steps: first, the total change between the baseline and the projected year is calculated; second, this amount is assigned to households within each region.

To obtain the total change in international remittances, the target amount is estimated as the product of the total value of remittances in a baseline using actual microdata and the growth rate from macro projections (δ_r) (equation (2.36)). Then the total value of remittances considering population growth is calculated (equation (2.37)); and then the difference is taken (equation (2.38)).

$$R_1^I = \left[\sum_h \eta_h^I w_h \right] (1 + \delta_r) \qquad (2.36)$$

$$\hat{R}_0^I = \sum_h \eta_h^I \hat{w}_h \qquad (2.37)$$

$$\Delta R^I = R_1^I - \hat{R}_0^I. \qquad (2.38)$$

This result can be positive, negative, or zero, and its sign defines the assignment rule applied in the second step of the method. Thus, if the total change is positive ($\Delta R^I > 0$), the increase in remittances will be allocated as follows:

- Across regions, remittances are allocated proportionally to the baseline regional distribution (rank-preserving regional transformation).
- Among households within regions, recipient households are selected at random and given a remittances transfer equivalent in real terms to the weighted average remittances transfer in that region in the baseline year, with the weighted *number* of total transfers to be made within each region equal to the total amount of additional remittances to be distributed, divided by the baseline average value.

As a result of this process, the overall distribution of remittances across regions remains unchanged although there is an increase in the number of recipient households.

When the change is negative ($\Delta R^I < 0$), recipient households are scaled down to the point at which the total value of remittances in the country—considering population growth—meets the total target.[6]

Domestic Remittances, Income on Capital, and Other Financial Income

Domestic remittances (r_h^D) and rents, interest, and dividends on capital (k_h) are assumed to grow at the same rate as real GDP, and the two-step method described above is followed, but with a simpler assignment rule. The first step consists of obtaining the total change in domestic remittances and capital income between the baseline and projected year, initially focusing only on domestic remittances. The target amount is estimated to be the product of the total value of remittances in the baseline using actual microdata and the growth rate of the total economy (δ_{GDP}) (equation (2.39)). The total value of remittances is calculated considering population growth (equation (2.40)); and then the difference is taken (equation (2.41)):

$$R_1^D = \left[\sum_h r_h^D w_h \right] (1 + \delta_{GDP}) \qquad (2.39)$$

$$\widehat{R}_0^D = \sum_h r_h^D \hat{w}_h \qquad (2.40)$$

$$\Delta R^D = R_1^D - \widehat{R}_0^D. \qquad (2.41)$$

For non-labor income coming from capital and other financial sources, the total change is estimated using equations (2.42)–(2.44):

$$K_1 = \left[\sum_h k_h w_h \right] (1 + \delta_{GDP}) \qquad (2.42)$$

$$\widehat{K}_0 = \sum_h k_h \hat{w}_h \qquad (2.43)$$

$$\Delta K = K_1 - \widehat{K}_0. \qquad (2.44)$$

In the second step, a simple rule of rescaling up or down the total amount of household recipients is applied when the total change in domestic remittances is positive ($\Delta R^D > 0$) or negative ($\Delta R^D < 0$), respectively. The same method is used for positive ($\Delta K > 0$) or negative ($\Delta K < 0$) movements in capital and other financial sources.

Other Non-Labor Income

Other non-labor income sources, such as social transfers or any other kinds of private transfers (tr_h), as well as other non-labor income (z_h), remain constant in real terms at the baseline levels.

Assessment

The impact assessment is the process by which the information on individual employment status and labor income, as well as on non-labor income at the household level, is used to generate income or consumption distributions and to calculate various poverty and distributional measures that can then be used to compare different scenarios.

New per Capita Household Income

The first step calculates—based on all previous estimations—total household income by aggregating total labor income across all employed members and adding non-labor income, then uses information on household size to construct the per capita household income, as in equation (2.45):

$$\hat{y}_h = \frac{1}{n_h}\left[\sum_{i=1}^{n_h}\sum_{L=1}^{\Lambda}\sum_{j=0}^{J}\mathbb{1}\left[\breve{U}_{hi}^{Lj} = j\right]\hat{y}_{hi}^{Lj} + \hat{y}_{0h}\right]. \tag{2.45}$$

Price Adjustment

The ADePT Simulation Module also takes into account price projections to adjust the poverty line to reflect the difference in food and non-food inflation rates between the baseline and the projected year. Because the poverty line is typically anchored to a food basket that ensures a minimum calorie intake, for countries where food inflation is expected to be significantly different from general inflation between baseline and projected years, the baseline poverty line would not be enough for a household to meet the basic food requirements in the projected year.

The first step is to express the food and non-food price indices in baseline-year terms. Second, an adjustment factor for the poverty line for each scenario or year is calculated as in equation (2.46):

$$\delta_z = \left(\frac{CPI^F \; w_z^F + CPI^{NF} \; w_z^{NF}}{CPI^T} \right) - 1, \qquad (2.46)$$

in which CPI^F = consumer price index for food,
CPI^{NF} = consumer price index for non-food
CPI^T = consumer price index total
w_z^F = weight of the food basket in the poverty line (z)
w_z^{NF} = weight of the non-food basket in the poverty line (z)

Third, the ADePT Simulation Module corrects the poverty line simply as equation (2.47):

$$z_1 = z_0 \left(1 + \delta_z\right). \qquad (2.47)$$

Mapping Income to Consumption Space

For those countries where poverty is defined according to consumption instead of income, household incomes are transformed into predicted consumption levels using the consumption income ratio for each household from the baseline year (equation (2.48)):

$$\hat{c}_h = \hat{y}_h \; \frac{c_h^0}{y_h^0}. \qquad (2.48)$$

Notes

1. Notice that although specific models for salaried and nonsalaried workers could be estimated based on the microdata from the household survey, this information is generally not available from the macro side so the models could not be used. Macroeconomic projections are calculated mainly for aggregate economic sectors such as agriculture, industry, and services instead of wage or self-employed, or formal and informal sectors.
2. Bourguignon and Ferreira (2005) say that this interpretation is not fully justified because occupational choices may actually be constrained by the demand side of the market, as in the case of selective rationing, rather than by individual preferences.
3. For simplicity, we temporarily remove the L superscript, which refers to education level of the individual.

4. This section is based on Wittenberg (2010).

5. This assumption could be easily removed by not including this variable in the analysis or by redefining it according to what the user needs.

6. The ADePT Simulation Module provides two methods to simulate this non-labor income component: the simple approach, which only rescales up or down all recipient households, and the random approach, which considers increases in the number of recipients when there is an increase in the amount of remittances.

References

Bourguignon, F., and F. Ferreira. 2005. "Decomposing Changes in the Distribution of Household Incomes: Methodological Aspects." In *The Microeconomics of Income Distribution Dynamics in East Asia and Latin America*, edited by F. Bourguignon, F. Ferreira, and N. Lustig. Washington, DC: Oxford University Press and World Bank.

Bourguignon, F., A. S. Robilliard, and S. Robinson. 2005. "Representative versus Real Households in the Macroeconomic Modeling of Inequality." In *Frontiers in Applied General Equilibrium Modeling: In Honor of Herbert Scarf*, edited by T. J. Kehoe, T. N. Srinivasan, and J. Whalley. Cambridge, U.K.: Cambridge University Press.

Bourguignon, F., M. Fournier, and M. Gurgand. 2007. "Selection Bias Corrections Based on the Multinomial Logit Model: Monte Carlo Comparisons." *Journal of Economic Surveys* 21 (1): 174–205.

McFadden, D. 1974. "Conditional Logit Analysis of Qualitative Choice Behavior." In *Frontiers in Econometrics*, edited by P. Zarembka. New York: Academic Press.

Mincer, J. 1974. *Schooling, Experience and Earnings*. New York: Columbia University Press for the National Bureau of Economic Research.

Train, K., and W. Wilson. 2008. "Estimation on Stated-Preference Experiments Constructed from Revealed-Preference Choices." *Transportation Research Part B: Methodological* 42 (3): 191–203.

Wittenberg, M. 2010. "An Introduction to Maximum Entropy and Minimum Cross-Entropy Estimation Using Stata." *The Stata Journal* 10 (3): 315–30.

Wooldridge, J. 2002. *Econometric Analysis of Cross Section and Panel Data*. Cambridge, Massachusetts: MIT Press.

PART II

Using the ADePT Simulation Module

Chapter 3

Introduction to Use of the ADePT Simulation Module

The ADePT Simulation Module is one of several modules in the ADePT platform, which also includes Poverty and Inequality, Labor, Social Protection, Gender, and Health, among other modules. Most modules generate standardized tables and charts summarizing the results of distributional analyses of household survey data.

The ADePT Simulation Module differs from other modules by its outputs and estimation complexity. The main output is a simulated database that can be used to perform further poverty, inequality, and employment analyses using complementary ADePT modules and other statistical packages such as Stata or SPSS. This output is supplemented with diagnostic tables reflecting the quality of the simulations and documenting the changes and transitions that occurred. The workflow can be divided into three steps: inputs to the simulation, outputs from the simulation, and analysis of outputs (figure 3.1).

Part II consists of four additional chapters. Chapter 4 describes how to produce the two sets of inputs required for the simulation: macroeconomic projections and microeconomic variables (microdata). It also explains how to enter these inputs into the module and the different options available for tailoring the simulation. It offers guidelines for addressing some difficulties that may arise during the process.

Chapter 5 focuses on outputs generated by this module. It discusses not only key tables and charts but also the output datasets and how these datasets could be used in postsimulation analysis.

Figure 3.1: How the ADePT Simulation Module Works

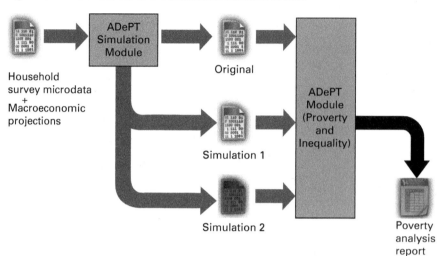

Household
survey microdata
+
Macroeconomic
projections

Original

Simulation 1

Simulation 2

ADePT
Module
(Proverty
and
Inequality)

Poverty
analysis
report

Chapter 6 contains a set of condensed instructions that simplify the detail of chapter 4.

Part II ends with a problem set in chapter 7, with solutions for the first question of each exercise. These exercises are focused mainly on how different parts of the simulation process work independently of each other.

Preparing and Entering Data

Data requirements for the ADePT Simulation Module are fairly straightforward. However, ADePT has only basic data manipulation capability, hence the data often need to be prepared *before* they are loaded into the module. The process involves generating two sets of inputs: macroeconomic projections and microeconomic variables (microdata). The following sections describe each step necessary to create or obtain proper inputs required for the simulation. They also explain how to load these inputs into the module and the options available for tailoring the simulation. Subsections give brief guidelines for solving some problems that might be faced during the process.[1]

Macroeconomic Data

The macroeconomic input data are divided into two sets: population growth and macroeconomic projections. The macroeconomic projections include four different kinds of inputs: total and sector output growth, total and sector employment growth, international transfers, and food and non-food inflation.

A few main definitions must be clarified before describing each step of the input generating process. These are typical of most macroeconomic inputs:

- *Baseline year* usually corresponds to the last available household or labor force survey in the country. For instance, if the last available

Household Income and Expenditure Survey is 2006 for the country of interest, then the baseline year is 2006.

- *Growth rates* refer to the percentage change between the baseline year (t_0) and projected year (t_1), as in equation (4.1):

$$\Delta x = \frac{x_{t1} - x_{t0}}{x_{t0}}, \qquad (4.1)$$

in which x could be any macroeconomic input, such as population, total GDP, or employment, among others. For instance, consider the assessment of the impact of a macro shock in 2013 for a country. The growth rate of total output (GDP) is defined between 2006 and 2013 as

$$\Delta GDP = \frac{GDP13 - GDP06}{GDP06}.$$

All monetary macroeconomic data must be expressed in real terms.

Population Growth Data

The ADePT Simulation Module also offers the option of including population growth in its predictions. It uses growth projections (disaggregated by gender and age group) between the baseline and the projected year. This process fully accounts for demographic changes that would affect the size and composition of the labor force, and through that, the estimates of per capita income or consumption. In simple terms, this process reweights the households in the baseline data to replicate demographic changes predicted by population projections.[2] This is particularly relevant in countries with high fertility rates and a relatively long time between the baseline and projected year.

Population projections are generally available from a country's national statistical office or the UN World Population Prospects.[3] The idea is to estimate growth rates between the baseline and the projected year by age and gender. However, an exact match between the available population projections and the baseline and projected years we want to predict is not typically found. For instance, the UN projections are spaced five years apart—2005, 2010, 2015, and so on—while the baseline and projected years in the example are 2006 and 2013, respectively.

Generating Population Growth Rate Data

One way to produce these inputs is to interpolate the data between two available projected years, generate the total population for those particular years of interest, then estimate growth rates by age and gender between the baseline and projected years. Suppose the user wants to estimate the population growth rates for Mexico between 2006 and 2013. Table 4.1 presents population projections by gender and age group under the medium variant scenario from UN World Population Prospects, in columns (1) through (6).

1. First, the annual growth rates by gender and age group are estimated for both intervals 2005 to 2010 and 2010 to 2015. As an example, for males columns (7) and (9) are estimated using the information in columns (3) and (1) using the formula in equation (4.2):

$$\Delta p^a = \left(\frac{P_{t1}}{P_{t0}} \right)^{1/(t1-t0)} - 1 = \left(\frac{\text{column}(3)}{\text{column}(1)} \right)^{1/(2010-2005)} - 1. \qquad (4.2)$$

2. Then equation (4.3) is used to calculate total population for 2006 (column 11) and 2013 (column 13) using 2005 and 2010, respectively, as initial years:

$$P_{06} = P_{05} \times \left(1 + \Delta p^a \right)^{(2006-2005)} = \text{column}(1) \times \left(1 + \text{column}(7) \right). \qquad (4.3)$$

3. Finally, equation (4.4) is used to calculate population growth rates by gender and age group between the baseline (2006) and projected years (2013), yielding the inputs in column (15) of table 4.1:

$$\Delta p = \frac{P_{t1}}{P_{t0}} - 1 = \frac{\text{column}(13)}{\text{column}(11)} - 1. \qquad (4.4)$$

Entering Population Growth Rate Data

The ADePT Simulation Module divides the process of entering population growth rate data into two steps. The first step consists in dividing the total age range of population projections into equal intervals. In the **Population projections** tab, select the **From** and **To** age bounds and the **Interval** (figure 4.1), then click the **Set** button.

Table 4.1: Population Growth Projections – Mexico
(thousands)

	2005		2010		2015		Δ 2010 vs 2005	
Age	Male (1)	Female (2)	Male (3)	Female (4)	Male (5)	Female (6)	Male (7)	Female (8)
0–9	11,214	10,806	11,361	10,911	11,036	10,575	0.003	0.002
10–19	10,765	10,719	10,932	10,738	10,932	10,662	0.003	0.000
20–29	9,095	9,454	9,173	9,634	9,895	10,134	0.002	0.004
30–39	7,984	8,280	8,539	8,866	8,495	8,903	0.014	0.014
40–49	5,741	6,024	6,576	6,941	7,654	8,036	0.028	0.029
50–59	3,717	3,892	4,605	4,920	5,406	5,796	0.044	0.048
60–69	2,305	2,419	2,664	2,815	3,321	3,594	0.029	0.031
70–79	1,274	1,605	1,483	1,748	1,756	1,975	0.031	0.017
80–89	412	610	531	788	657	951	0.052	0.053
90+	59	106	70	130	97	183	0.035	0.042

	Δ 2015 vs 2010		2006		2013		Δ 2013 vs 2006	
Age	Male (9)	Female (10)	Male (11)	Female (12)	Male (13)	Female (14)	Male (15)	Female (16)
0–9	−0.006	−0.006	11,243.2	10,826.9	11,165.0	10,708.0	−0.007	−0.011
10–19	0.000	−0.001	10,798.2	10,722.8	10,932.0	10,692.0	0.012	−0.003
20–29	0.015	0.010	9,110.5	9,489.7	9,600.0	9,931.0	0.054	0.046
30–39	−0.001	0.001	8,092.0	8,394.0	8,513.0	8,888.2	0.052	0.059
40–49	0.031	0.030	5,899.1	6,197.2	7,203.0	7,578.7	0.221	0.223
50–59	0.033	0.033	3,879.7	4,078.8	5,070.0	5,428.3	0.307	0.331
60–69	0.045	0.050	2,372.7	2,493.5	3,041.0	3,259.4	0.282	0.307
70–79	0.034	0.025	1,313.3	1,632.6	1,641.0	1,880.9	0.250	0.152
80–89	0.044	0.038	433.4	642.1	603.4	882.1	0.392	0.374
90+	0.067	0.071	61.1	110.4	85.13	159.61	0.394	0.445

Source: Estimations based on UN World Population Prospects 2010 revision.
Note: Δ = change. Age groups are added for presentation purposes. See text for calculation of change columns.

Figure 4.1: Population Projections – Age Brackets

Once the age intervals have been defined, the next step is to enter the population growth rates previously estimated. The **Males** and **Females** inputs use data from the last two columns of table 4.1 (figure 4.2). If the user decides to modify the age intervals, then the user must reset the parameters previously defined and introduce the new ones, which will create a new grid.

Figure 4.2: Population Projections – Growth Rates Inputs

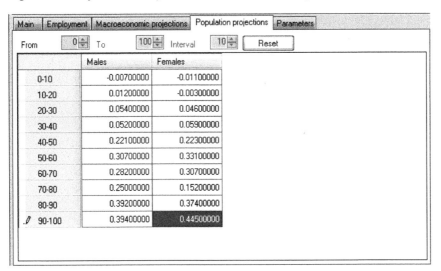

Generating and Entering Macroeconomic Data

This section explains how to use macroeconomic projections that could be generated with a macroeconomic model, or computable general equilibrium model, to produce inputs for the simulation.[4] However, all of these parameters are optional and can be freely manipulated. Zero indicates no growth in that particular parameter. Be aware that consistent macroeconomic inputs will likely produce reasonable microeconomic simulations. The following subsections describe four input types: changes in total and sector output, total and sector employment, remittances from abroad, and prices.

Generating Changes in Total and Sector Output

Among the most important inputs to the simulation are the growth rates for the total economy and its main economic sectors, either for each simulated scenario (scenario 1, scenario 2, and so on) of the same projected year, or for only one scenario for each year. Note that these growth rates must be estimated based on output data expressed in baseline year prices. These rates represent the percentage change between the baseline and the projected year.

Table 4.2: GDP Total and Economic-Sector Growth Projections – The Philippines
(in real terms)

Sector	2006 (1)	2009 Scenario 1 (2)	2009 Scenario 2 (3)	2010 Scenario 1 (4)	2010 Scenario 2 (5)	Δ 2009 vs 2006 (percent) Scenario 1 (6)	Δ 2009 vs 2006 (percent) Scenario 2 (7)	Δ 2010 vs 2006 (percent) Scenario 1 (8)	Δ 2010 vs 2006 (percent) Scenario 2 (9)
Total	1,276,156	1,485,526	1,438,056	1,559,412	1,482,592	16.4	12.7	22.2	16.2
Agriculture	239,777	267,215	262,312	275,274	268,136	11.4	9.4	19.5	14.1
Manufacturing	305,663	342,490	308,899	356,874	311,988	12.0	1.1	28.0	6.2
Other Industries	109,152	144,746	152,108	154,507	165,122	32.6	39.4	47.9	63.7
Services	621,564	731,075	714,736	772,757	737,345	17.6	15.0	39.5	20.5

Source: Habib et al. 2010.
Note: Δ = change.

Assume the user wants to predict some distributional impacts of a specific macroeconomic shock for 2009 and 2010 given that the last available household survey for the Philippines is 2006 (table 4.2). The baseline year is 2006, and all output data must be in 2006 real terms. In this case, we have two scenarios for the same year: Scenario 1 represents the behavior of the economy if it remains on trend, and Scenario 2 corresponds to how the economy would react if there is a macroeconomic shock. Once projections are estimated using a macroeconomic model or computable general equilibrium (CGE),[5] the objective is to obtain columns (6) through (9) applying equation (4.1).

Entering Growth-of-Sector-GDP Data

The ADePT Simulation Module accepts all macro inputs in the **Macroeconomic projections** tab, including not only GDP projections but also employment, prices, and international remittances (figure 4.3). This section focuses only on those columns corresponding to the **Growth of sector GDP** and the **Growth of total GDP** fields. The data entry process can be separated into several steps.

First, determine which type of assessment is desired: "before versus after" (Type II from figure 1.2) or "with and without" shock (Type I from figure 1.2). This is set using the **Specify second scenario** option in the **Macroeconomic projections** tab (figure 4.4).

Choosing this option activates all columns corresponding to this kind of assessment, enabling all inputs for each scenario of the same year to be included, as shown in figure 4.5:

Figure 4.3: Macroeconomic Inputs – Output Growth Rates

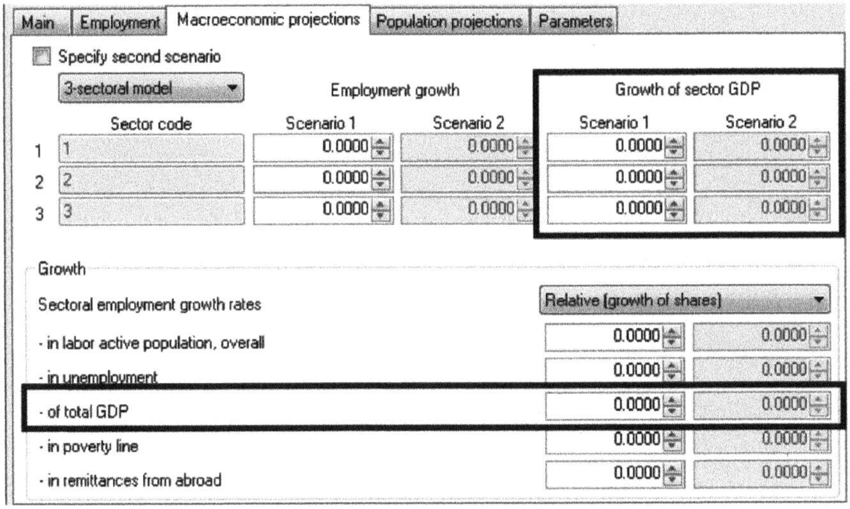

Figure 4.4: Macroeconomic Inputs – Specify Second Scenario

Figure 4.5: Macroeconomic Inputs – Second Scenario Enabled

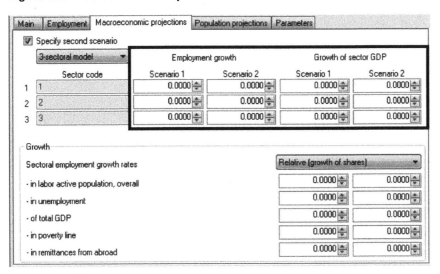

The next step is to define the number of sectors to include in the assessment. In this example, there are four economic sectors; agriculture, manufacturing, other industries, and services. The ADePT Simulation Module only allows for two options: either three or four economic sectors, set just below the **Specify second scenario** option. Note that these divisions could be related to different sets of economic sector classifications such as those just identified or, for example, formal tradable, formal nontradable, and informal. These classifications depend on the availability of macroeconomic projections for such divisions as well as the identification of the same divisions in the microdata.

The last step consists of entering GDP growth rates by economic sector in the **Growth of sector GDP** columns for each scenario and for the specified year. For instance, assume the year we want to project is 2010 in Scenario 1 and Scenario 2 for four economic sectors in the Philippines (table 4.2). All growth rates must first be expressed in *decimals* instead of *percentages*. That is, if the GDP growth rate for Manufacturing (sector code 2) between the baseline (2006) and the projected year (2010) in Scenario 1 is 28 percent, the user must enter 0.28 (figure 4.6). Additionally, the *order* of the macro sectors matter and must correspond to the micro sector's order, and vice versa. For instance, if sector code number 1 is assigned to agriculture in the macroeconomic data, it must be 1 in the microdata.

Figure 4.6: Macroeconomic Inputs – Total and Sector Output Growth Rates

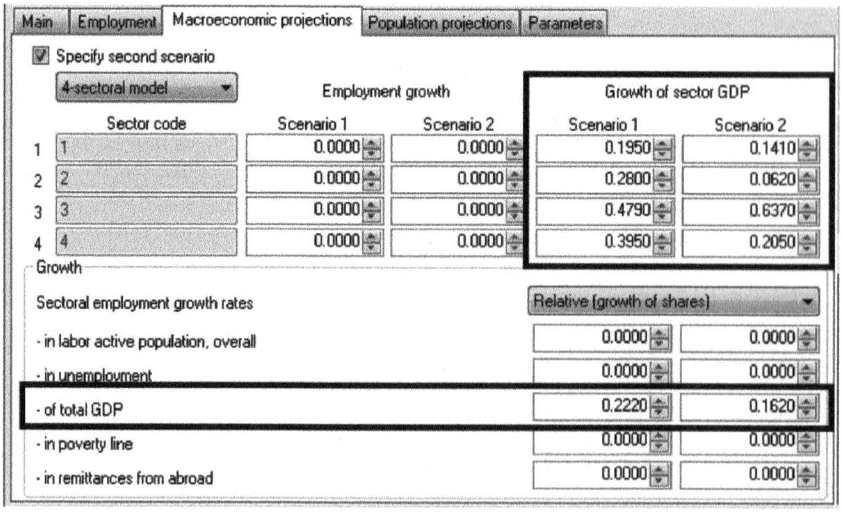

The growth rate for the total economy is located in the third row of the **Growth** panel (below panels for the sector growth rates for Employment and GDP) (figure 4.6). In the **Growth** panel, the left column refers to Scenario 1 and the right column to Scenario 2. As with the sector growth rates, this data must be expressed in decimals instead of percentages.

Generating Total and Sector Changes in Employment and Labor Force Participation Data

One deficiency observed across countries is the lack of employment and labor force participation projections. These inputs are relevant in the simulation because they determine how the working population is going to be reallocated between labor statuses as a result of the shock. Different methods allow these inputs to be generated, varying from sophisticated macro models based on CGE or investment savings and liquidity preference–money supply,[6] to simple ones based on an employment-output elasticity approach.

This section focuses on explaining how to produce these inputs based on employment-output elasticity approach. This approach assumes that changes in labor market conditions are proportional to changes in output, but (among other drawbacks) it does not consider substitution effects between workers of different skill levels within and between sectors. The advantages of this method include its simplicity as well as its low data demands.[7]

To project the labor market structure, two sets of elasticities could be estimated: the employment-output elasticity by economic sector and the activity-output elasticity. Employment-output elasticities relate changes in employment in a specific sector (for example, agriculture, industry, or services) to changes in GDP in constant prices in that specific sector between the same years. The activity-output elasticity associates changes in the activity rate for the working population to changes in total GDP. Note that the list of elements in the first set of elasticities depends on how many sectors are in the economy. However, the ADePT Simulation Module only allows for three or four economic sectors, as mentioned previously.

It is important to clarify that the inputs for the simulation are the main goal, and the estimation of these sets of elasticities is the means for getting those inputs. The process for obtaining the total and sector changes in employment for the simulation can be split into two main steps: the first step calculates the employment-output elasticity based on past data; the second step calculates the proper inputs based on growth rates between baseline and projections.

Estimating Employment-Output Elasticity by Economic Sector and Estimating Activity-Output Elasticity

To estimate elasticity, we first need to fulfill one set of data requirements for labor market and GDP. From the labor market data viewpoint, the method requires information in two dimensions:

- *Structure* of the labor market, such as employment (total and by the three or four sectors), total active population, and total working-age population[8]
- *Time*: historical data for a minimum of two years

The method also requires GDP data in the same dimensions:

- *Structure*: total GDP and GDP by sector
- *Time*: historical data for a minimum of two years, and projections

We start by estimating employment-output elasticity by economic sector. Note that employment sectors and GDP sectoral disaggregation must correspond to each other as well as correspond for historical years. The employment-output elasticity for a particular economic sector (for example, manufacturing) is the percentage change in employment in that sector with respect to a 1 percent change in sector GDP (equation (4.5)).
Formally,

$$\eta_t^S = \frac{\Delta\% \; Emp_t^S}{\Delta\% \; GDP_t^S},$$ (4.5)

in which S = economic sector (for example, agriculture, industry, services)
  t = time with $t = 2$
  $\Delta\%$ = percentage change with respect to the first year

These elasticities are computed for $T-1$ years to get a time series by economic sector. The simple average across time can then be calculated and can be considered the link between GDP and employment for a particular economic sector (equation (4.6)); formally,

$$\eta^S = \frac{\sum_{t=2}^{T} \eta_t^S}{(T-1)}.$$ (4.6)

For instance, for the Philippines example, we first construct the time series for employment and GDP by economic sector for 2003–08 (tables 4.3 and 4.4). Then we calculate the percentage change for every year for both series and we calculate the ratio between them for each year. Finally, we calculate the simple average.

These parameters may fluctuate significantly over the years and the Philippines was not an exception. Sometimes, using past relationships between employment and GDP might not be representative of the asymmetries in labor market behavior during downturns and booms, as well as in the short and medium terms, regardless of which econometric technique (that is, simple average or more sophisticated methods based on time series analysis) is employed for their estimation. For instance, during the 2008–09 financial crisis, data available from Mexico's labor force survey (Encuesta Nacional de Ocupación y Empleo) for the first quarters of 2009 and 2010 suggested that employment levels exhibited a certain degree of downward

Table 4.3: Philippines Employment
(population 15 years old and older; thousands)

	Employment				Change in employment (percent)			
	Agriculture	Manufacturing	Other industries	Services	Agriculture	Manufacturing	Other industries	Services
2003	11,219	2,941	1,899	14,574	—	—	—	—
2004	11,381	3,061	1,938	15,233	1.4	4.1	2.0	4.5
2005	11,603	3,077	1,947	15,659	2.0	0.5	0.5	2.8
2006	11,691	3,060	1,933	15,952	0.8	−0.6	−0.7	1.9
2007	11,780	3,062	2,056	16,662	0.8	0.1	6.3	4.5
2008	12,034	2,931	2,122	17,002	2.2	−4.3	3.2	2.0

Source: National Statistics Office of the Philippines.
Note: — = Not available.

Table 4.4: Philippines GDP by Sector
(constant prices)

	GDP				Change in sectoral GDP (percent)			
	Agriculture	Manufacturing	Other industries	Services	Agriculture	Manufacturing	Other industries	Services
2003	215,273	263,255	100,231	506,313	—	—	—	—
2004	226,417	278,624	103,795	545,458	5.2	5.8	3.6	7.7
2005	230,954	293,334	103,548	583,616	2.0	5.3	−0.2	7.0
2006	239,777	305,663	109,152	621,564	3.8	4.2	5.4	6.5
2007	251,311	315,709	127,358	672,115	4.8	3.3	16.7	8.1
2008	259,406	329,317	135,700	694,529	3.2	4.3	6.6	3.3

Source: National Statistics Office of the Philippines.
Note: — = Not available.

stickiness, compared with what would have been projected on the basis of medium-term trends.[9]

Once the employment-output elasticity is estimated, the next step is to calculate projected employment by economic sector. Two main inputs are needed: employment-output elasticity by sector (already calculated, as in table 4.5) and GDP projections. See equations (4.7) and (4.8).

$$\eta^S = \frac{\Delta\% \ Emp^S_{T+1}}{\Delta\% \ GDP^S_{T+1}} \Rightarrow \Delta\% \ Emp^S_{T+1} = \eta^S * \Delta\% \ GDP^S_{T+1} \qquad (4.7)$$

$$Emp^S_{T+1} = Emp^S_T \times \left(1 + \Delta\% \ Emp^S_{T+1}\right). \qquad (4.8)$$

For example, assume we want to project the population employed in services for 2009 in the Philippines. The last available data for employment is 2008, with 17 million people employed in services (table 4.3). We already calculated the average employment-output elasticity for this sector, which is about 0.49 (table 4.5). The projected percentage change in Scenario 1 between 2008 and 2009 for GDP in services is 5.3 percent (tables 4.2 and 4.4). Following the previous formula and the information available:

$$S = Service$$
$$T = 2008$$
$$\eta^S = 0.49$$
$$\Delta\% \ GDP^S_{09} = 5.3$$
$$Emp^S_{08} = 17 \text{ million people}$$

Table 4.5: Employment-Output Elasticity – The Philippines
(by economic sector)

	$\eta = \Delta\%$ employment $/\Delta\%$ GDP			
	Agriculture	Manufacturing	Other industries	Services
2003	—	—	—	—
2004	0.278	0.699	0.566	0.585
2005	0.977	0.099	−2.060	0.400
2006	0.198	−0.133	−0.130	0.288
2007	0.158	0.027	0.379	0.547
2008	0.668	−0.992	0.495	0.613
Average η^S	**0.456**	**−0.060**	**−0.150**	**0.486**

Source: Authors' estimations.
Note: Δ = change; — = Not available.

Now employment in services can be projected using equations (4.9) and (4.10):

$$\Delta\% \, Emp_{09}^S = 0.49 \times 5.3\% = 2.6\% \qquad (4.9)$$

$$Emp_{09}^S = 17 \times (1 + 2.6\%) = 17.44 \text{ million people} \qquad (4.10)$$

This procedure is repeated for each economic sector and projected year or scenario (table 4.6). Total employment is the sum of the total population employed in the different sectors.

The next elasticity necessary to complete the projected labor market structure is the activity-output elasticity. This elasticity is defined as the ratio between the percentage change of the activity rate[10] and the percentage change of total GDP between the same years. Formally, we calculate the elasticity for $T-1$ periods and take the simple average across time as mentioned before:[11]

$$\eta_t^A = \frac{\Delta\% \, Act_t}{\Delta\% \, GDP_t} \qquad (4.11)$$

$$\eta^A = \frac{\sum_{t=2}^{T} \eta_t^A}{(T-1)}. \qquad (4.12)$$

Table 4.6: Employment Projections by Economic Sector – The Philippines
(population 15 years old and older; thousands)

		Employment			
	Total	*Agriculture*	*Manufacturing*	*Other industries*	*Services*
2003	30,634	11,219	2,941	1,899	14,574
2004	31,612	11,381	3,061	1,938	15,233
2005	32,286	11,603	3,077	1,947	15,659
2006	32,636	11,691	3,060	1,933	15,952
2007	33,560	11,780	3,062	2,056	16,662
2008	34,090	12,034	2,931	2,122	17,002
Scenario 1					
2009	34,662	12,199	2,924	2,101	17,438
2010	35,284	12,366	2,917	2,080	17,921
Scenario 2					
2009	34,364	12,095	2,942	2,084	17,243
2010	34,723	12,218	2,940	2,057	17,508

Source: Habib et al. 2010.

Table 4.7: Activity-Output Elasticity – The Philippines

	Population (1)	Labor force (2)	Activity rate (3)=(2)/(1)	Total GDP constant prices(4)	(5)= Δ%(3)	(6)= Δ%(4)	$\eta^{At}=$ Δ(5)/(6)
2003	51,793	34,571	0.667	1,085,072	—	—	—
2004	53,144	35,862	0.675	1,154,294	1.1	6.4	0.172
2005	54,388	35,381	0.651	1,211,452	−3.6	5.0	−0.727
2006	55,230	35,370	0.640	1,276,156	−1.6	5.3	−0.291
2007	56,565	36,213	0.640	1,366,493	0.0	7.1	−0.005
2008	57,848	36,806	0.636	1,418,952	−0.6	3.8	−0.161
					Average η^A		**−0.202**

Sources: Habib et al. 2010; estimations from [SOURCE] data.
Note: Δ = change; — = Not available.
$\eta = ?$

The results are shown in table 4.7.

Now the activity rates for each year or scenario can be projected using the same reasoning as for employment. An example for 2009 under Scenario 1 is presented in the following:

$T = 2008$

$\eta^A = -0.20$

$\Delta\% \ GDP_{09} = (1485.5/1418.9) - 1 \times 100 = 4.7$

$Act_{08} = 0.636$ percent

Then, equations (4.13) and (4.14) are used:

$$\Delta\% \ Act_{09} = -0.20 \times 4.7\% = -0.9\% \tag{4.13}$$

$$Act_{09} = 0.64 \times (1 + (-0.9\%)) = 0.63. \tag{4.14}$$

The next step is to project the total labor force population by year or scenario. First, the total population projections have to be obtained for each year or scenario and then must be multiplied by the projected activity rates (table 4.8). Note that population projections for the working-age range (between 15 and 64 years old, or 15 years old and older) come from the previous "Population Growth" section in this chapter.

There are two labor statuses left that complete the projected labor market structure: unemployment and inactivity. These two categories will give the user complete information about how reasonable the projected labor market structures are according to the current situation of the country under study. Table 4.9 shows an example for the Philippines. It can be seen, for

Table 4.8: Labor Force Population – The Philippines
(population 15 years old and older; thousands)

	Population (1)	*Labor force (2)*	*Activity rate (3) = (2)/(1)*
2003	51,793	34,571	0.667
2004	53,144	35,862	0.675
2005	54,388	35,381	0.651
2006	55,230	35,370	0.640
2007	56,565	36,213	0.640
2008	57,848	36,806	0.636
Scenario1			
2009	59,342	37,398	0.630
2010	60,880	37,981	0.624
Scenario 2			
2009	59,342	37,653	0.635
2010	60,880	38,387	0.631

Sources: Habib et al. 2010; estimations from [SOURCE] data.

Table 4.9: Labor Market Structure – The Philippines

	1. In thousands								
	TOTAL	Inactive	Active	Unemployment	Employment	Agriculture	Manufacturing	Other industries	Services
2003	51,793	17,222	34,571	3,936	30,635	11,219	2,941	1,899	14,574
2004	53,144	17,282	35,862	4,249	31,613	11,381	3,061	1,938	15,233
2005	54,388	19,007	35,381	3,068	32,313	11,603	3,077	1,947	15,659
2006	55,230	19,860	35,370	2,734	32,636	11,691	3,060	1,933	15,952
2007	56,565	20,352	36,213	2,653	33,560	11,780	3,062	2,056	16,662
2008	57,848	21,043	36,806	2,716	34,090	12,034	2,931	2,122	17,002
Scenario 1									
2009	59,342	21,944	37,398	2,736	34,662	12,199	2,924	2,101	17,438
2010	60,880	22,899	37,981	2,697	35,284	12,366	2,917	2,080	17,921
Scenario 2									
2009	59,342	21,689	37,653	3,289	34,364	12,095	2,942	2,084	17,243
2010	60,880	22,493	38,387	3,664	34,723	12,218	2,940	2,057	17,508

	2. Shares					
	Activity rate	Employment	Agriculture	Manufacturing	Other industries	Services	Unemployment rate
2003	66.75	88.62	36.62	9.60	6.20	47.57	11.38
2004	67.48	88.15	36.00	9.68	6.13	48.19	11.85
2005	65.05	91.33	35.91	9.52	6.03	48.46	8.67
2006	64.04	92.27	35.82	9.38	5.92	48.88	7.73
2007	64.02	92.67	35.10	9.12	6.12	49.65	7.33
2008	63.62	92.62	35.30	8.60	6.23	49.88	7.38
Scenario 1							
2009	63.02	92.68	35.19	8.44	6.06	50.31	7.32
2010	62.39	92.90	35.05	8.27	5.89	50.79	7.10
Scenario 2							
2009	63.45	91.26	35.20	8.56	6.06	50.18	8.74
2010	63.05	90.46	35.19	8.47	5.92	50.42	9.54

Sources: Habib et al. 2010; estimations from [SOURCE] data.

instance, that projected unemployment rates for 2009 and 2010 in Scenario 1 continue along the same trend. In the Scenario 2 section, the rates do not differ significantly from the historical series. However, the lessons learned from the Mexican case suggest that it is not sufficient to generate reasonable projections; available real-time labor market information must also be taken into account. Sometimes past relationships between output and employment are not informative enough about the current situation.

Generating Employment Data

The last step generates the growth rates between the baseline and projected year(s) or scenarios (Scenario 1 and Scenario 2) for activity, unemployment, and employment, total and by sector. The ADePT Simulation Module provides two options for inputs: in *relative* terms or *absolute* terms. The first option refers to the growth rates of the *shares* of the labor structure. In other words, these are the growth rates of activity rate, unemployment rate, and the proportions of total individuals employed by economic sector. To obtain these growth rates of activity rates, we focus on panel 2 of table 4.9.

Now we calculate growth rates between baseline (2006) and projected years and scenarios. The inputs for the ADePT Simulation Module are the growth rates in table 4.10.

Table 4.10: Employment Growth Rates Based on Shares – The Philippines
(population 15 years old and older; percentages)

| | Activity rate | Shares | | | | | Unemployment rate |
		Employment	Agriculture	Manufacturing	Other industries	Services	
2006	64.04	92.27	35.82	9.38	5.92	48.88	7.73
Scenario 1							
2009	63.02	92.68	35.19	8.44	6.06	50.31	7.32
2010	62.39	92.90	35.05	8.27	5.89	50.79	7.10
Scenario 2							
2009	63.45	91.26	35.20	8.56	6.06	50.18	8.74
2010	63.05	90.46	35.19	8.47	5.92	50.42	9.54
Percent change							
Scenario 1							
2006–09	−1.59	0.45	−1.76	−10.01	2.31	2.93	−5.35
2006–10	−2.58	0.68	−2.16	−11.82	−0.51	3.91	−8.15
Scenario 2							
2006–09	−0.92	−1.09	−1.75	−8.67	2.35	2.66	13.01
2006–10	−1.54	−1.97	−1.78	−9.67	−0.01	3.16	23.47

Source: Habib et al. 2010; estimations from [SOURCE] data.

For the second option, we must calculate growth rates based on number of workers instead of shares. Using panel 1 in table 4.9, we compute growth rates for the labor structure between the baseline and the projected year for each scenario; the growth rates are shaded in table 4.11.

Entering Employment Data

We have now established the two scenarios and the number of economic sectors considered in the exercise. The next step consists of entering the employment growth rates by economic sectors in the **Employment growth** columns for each scenario and specific year (figure 4.7). For instance, the year we want to project is 2010 in Scenario 1 and Scenario 2 for four economic sectors in the Philippines (table 4.10). Before entering the figures from table 4.11 in the module, note that growth rates must be divided by 100. In other words, if the employment growth rate for agriculture between baseline (2006) and projected year (2010) in Scenario 1 is –2.16 percent, we must enter –0.0216. Also note that the *order* in which these inputs are entered in this sheet matters, and must match the order followed in the microeconomic data. For instance, if a sector's code 1 is assigned to agriculture in the macroeconomic data, it must correspond to agriculture in the microdata.

Table 4.11: Employment Growth Rates Based on Numbers of Workers – The Philippines
(population 15 years old and older; percentages)

		In thousands					
	Active population	Employment	Agriculture	Manufacturing	Other industries	Services	Unemployment
2006	35,370	32,636	11,691	3,060	1,933	15,952	2,734
Scenario 1							
2009	37,398	34,662	12,199	2,924	2,101	17,438	2,736
2010	37,981	35,284	12,366	2,917	2,080	17,921	2,697
Scenario 2							
2009	37,653	34,364	12,095	2,942	2,084	17,243	3,289
2010	38,387	34,723	12,218	2,940	2,057	17,508	3,664
Percent change							
Scenario 1							
2006–09	5.73	6.21	4.34	–4.42	8.67	9.32	0.07
2006–10	7.38	8.12	5.78	–4.66	7.57	12.35	–1.37
Scenario 2							
2006–09	6.46	5.30	3.46	–3.84	7.77	8.10	20.30
2006–10	8.53	6.40	4.50	–3.89	6.39	9.76	34.01

Sources: Habib et al. 2010; estimations from [SOURCE] data.

Figure 4.7: Macroeconomic Projections – Employment Relative Growth Rates

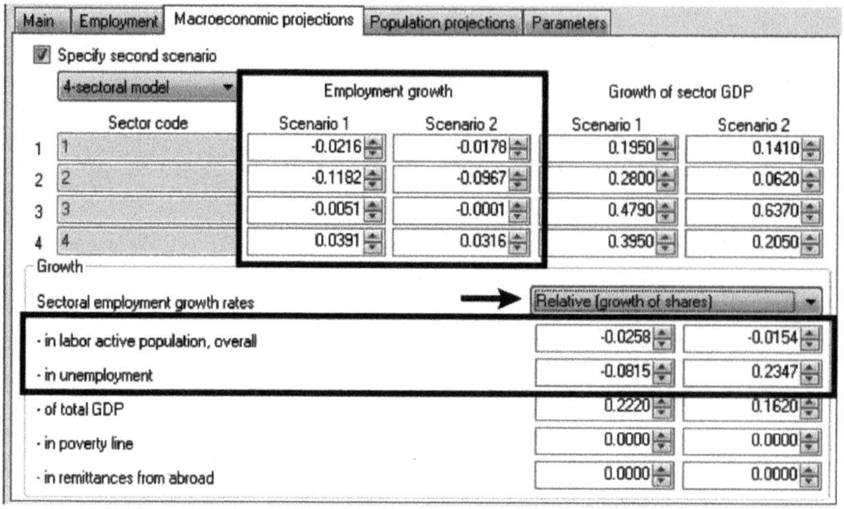

Growth rates for activity and unemployment rates between the baseline and the projected years are located within the group of other growth rates that also includes poverty line, remittances, and total GDP growth. These are the first and second fields of the **Growth** panel in which the left column refers to Scenario 1 and the right column to Scenario 2. Again, these must be expressed as decimals (figure 4.7).

To input growth rates based on *absolute* terms or number of workers, two main points mentioned before must be followed: *order* of economic sector in micro and macro data must match, and all growth rates must be divided by 100 if they are expressed as percentages. Note that it is not necessary to include the growth rate for **labor active population** as an input because it is obtained as a residual of total employment and unemployment changes (figure 4.8).

Generating Data on Changes in Remittances from Abroad

To create the macroeconomic input related to remittances from abroad, it is important first to express the remittances in real local currency units (LCUs), and then calculate the variation between baseline and projected year. One reason to convert this macro input into LCUs is that household surveys' international transfers are expressed in LCUs, and compatibility

Figure 4.8: Macroeconomic Projections – Employment Absolute Growth Rates

		Employment growth		Growth of sector GDP	
	Sector code	Scenario 1	Scenario 2	Scenario 1	Scenario 2
1	1	0.0578	0.0450	0.1950	0.1410
2	2	-0.0466	-0.0389	0.2800	0.0620
3	3	0.0757	0.0639	0.4790	0.6370
4	4	0.1235	0.0976	0.3950	0.2050

Main | Employment | Macroeconomic projections | Population projections | Parameters

☑ Specify second scenario

4-sectoral model ▼

Growth

	Scenario 1	Scenario 2
Sectoral employment growth rates → Absolute (growth of # of workers) ▼		
· in labor active population, overall	0.0000	0.0000
· in unemployment	-0.0137	0.3401
· of total GDP	0.2220	0.1620
· in poverty line	0.0000	0.0000
· in remittances from abroad	0.0000	0.0000

between macro and micro changes is important. Among other reasons, these transfers are affected by how exchange rates (ε) and internal inflation (that is, the consumer price index [CPI]) vary over time. For instance, even if there is an increase in the total amount of international remittances in nominal terms (in foreign currency units) during the period of the analysis, in real terms these transfers could show a decrease or no movement in their levels. In other words, what is relevant is their purchasing power. See equation (4.15):

$$R^R = \frac{R^N \varepsilon}{CPI},$$

(4.15)

in which R^R = remittances from abroad in real terms in LCU
R^N = remittances from abroad in nominal terms (foreign currency units)
ε = exchange rate
CPI = consumer price index

The ratio in equation (4.15) could produce different growth rate results in international transfers depending on how the numerator and denominator vary over time.

Once the macro international remittances data have been converted to real terms for the baseline and projected years, the next step is to calculate the growth rate between these periods for a particular scenario. For instance, we want to include in the analysis the growth rate of international transfers between baseline (2006) and projected year (2010) for the Philippines. We need information about domestic inflation, the exchange rate, and the volume of remittances from abroad in nominal terms for each year and scenario. We convert those into real terms and calculate growth rates (table 4.12).

Entering Data on Changes in Remittances from Abroad

After these calculations, we enter the growth rate between 2006 and 2010 for both scenarios in decimals in the last row of the **Growth** panel in the **Macroeconomic projections** tab (figure 4.9).

Two optional methods could also be used for allocating international remittances among households. These are explained in the "Other Options" section of this chapter.

Generating and Entering Price Data

The ADePT Simulation Module also considers price projections to adjust the poverty line to reflect the difference in food and non-food inflation rates

Table 4.12: Growth Rates of Remittances from Abroad – The Philippines

| | | Foreign exchange rate (Php/$) | Remittances | | |
| | CPI | | Million US$, nominal | Million Php, nominal | Million Php, real |
	(1)	(2)	(3)	(4) = (3)*(2)	(5) = (4)/(1)
2006	4.8	51.3	12,761	654,838	136,322
Scenario1					
2009	5.4	45.5	17,931	815,840	150,201
2010	5.7	46.0	19,544	899,038	157,636
Scenario2					
2009	5.6	49.0	17,084	837,112	150,733
2010	5.8	50.0	18,024	901,177	155,281
Percent change					
Scenario1					
2006–09			40.51	24.59	10.18
2006–10			53.15	37.29	15.64
Scenario2					
2006–09			33.87	27.84	10.57
2006–10			41.24	37.62	13.91

Sources: Habib et al. 2010; estimations from [SOURCE] data.
Note: 2006 = actual data; 2009 and 2010 are hypothetical projections. CPI = consumer price index; Php = Philippine pesos.

Figure 4.9: Macroeconomic Projections – International Remittances Growth Rate

	Sector code	Employment growth		Growth of sector GDP	
		Scenario 1	Scenario 2	Scenario 1	Scenario 2
1	1	-0.0216	-0.0178	0.1950	0.1410
2	2	-0.1182	-0.0967	0.2800	0.0620
3	3	-0.0051	-0.0001	0.4790	0.6370
4	4	0.0391	0.0316	0.3950	0.2050

Tabs: Main | Employment | Macroeconomic projections | Population projections | Parameters

☑ Specify second scenario
4-sectoral model

Growth

Sectoral employment growth rates	Relative (growth of shares)	
· in labor active population, overall	-0.0258	-0.0154
· in unemployment	-0.0815	0.2347
· of total GDP	0.2220	0.1620
· in poverty line	0.0000	0.0000
· in remittances from abroad	0.1564	0.1391

between the baseline and the projected year. The poverty line is typically anchored to a food basket that ensures a minimum calorie intake; therefore, for countries where food inflation is expected to be significantly different from general inflation between baseline and projected years, the baseline poverty line would not be sufficient for a household to meet the basic food requirements in the projected year.

To calculate this input, the following macro information is required: CPI: general, food, and non-food for baseline and projected years and scenarios; and the weights of the food and non-food baskets of the poverty line. The growth rate for the poverty line is estimated in two steps: first the base of the total, food, and non-food CPI is re-expressed in terms of the baseline year (table 4.13).

It is important to note that the ADePT Simulation Module does not allow more than one poverty line to be adjusted. Therefore, all poverty lines, income, and microdata welfare variables must be expressed in terms of one region or area poverty line. We recommend using as a reference the poverty line of an area that has a similar composition of food and non-food baskets to that of the CPI (for instance, the urban poverty line). In this sense, we are also "correcting" by spatial cost-of-living differences.[12]

**Table 4.13: Consumer Price Index – Total, Food, and Non-Food –
The Philippines**

	CPI (2000 = 100)			CPI (2006 = 100)		
	Total	Food	Non-food	Total (1)	Food (2)	Non-food (3)
2006	137.90	130.60	145.27	100.00	100.00	100.00
Scenario 1						
2009	156.02	148.43	163.61	113.14	113.65	112.63
2010	163.82	155.85	171.79	118.80	119.33	118.26
Scenario 2						
2009	160.01	160.24	159.77	116.03	122.70	109.99
2010	167.21	167.45	166.96	121.25	128.22	114.94

Sources: Habib et al. 2010; estimations from [SOURCE] data.
Note: CPI = consumer price index.

Second, the adjustment factor for the poverty line is calculated for each scenario or year according to equation (4.16):

$$\delta_z = \left(\frac{CPI^F \ w_z^F + CPI^{NF} \ w_z^{NF}}{CPI^T} \right) - 1, \qquad (4.16)$$

in which CPI^F = consumer price index for food
CPI^{NF} = consumer price index for non-food
CPI^T = consumer price index total
w_z^F = weight of the food basket in the poverty line (z)
w_z^{NF} = weight the non-food basket in the poverty line (z)

Given that the weights of the food and non-food baskets of the poverty line are equal to 57.41 and 42.59, respectively, for the National Capital Region of the Philippines, the adjustment factors for Scenario 1 and Scenario 2 are as shown in table 4.14.

Poverty line data are then entered in the **Growth** panel, in the **in poverty line** row (figure 4.10).

Microeconomic Inputs

The ADePT Simulation Module has only basic data manipulation capabilities, and the microdata need to be prepared *before* they are loaded into the software. ADePT uses a straightforward set of household or labor force

Table 4.14: Consumer Price Index Growth Rate – The Philippines

| | CPI (2006 = 100) | | | δ_z |
	General (1)	Food (2)	Non-Food (3)	(percent)
2006	100.00	100.00	100.00	
Scenario 1				
2009	113.14	113.65	112.63	0.07
2010	118.80	119.33	118.26	0.07
Scenario 2				
2009	116.03	122.70	109.99	1.08
2010	121.25	128.22	114.94	1.08

Sources: Habib et al. 2010; estimations from [SOURCE] data.
Note: CPI = consumer price index; δ_z = poverty line growth rate.

Figure 4.10: Macroeconomic Projections – Poverty Line Growth Rate

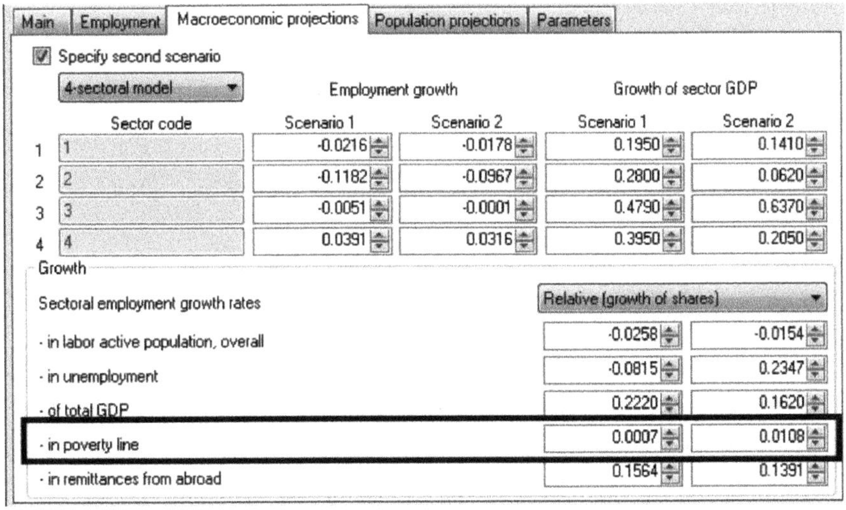

survey variables as micro inputs. These variables are grouped on the **Main** and **Employment** tabs. ADePT does not require predefined names to be specified in the input fields—any variable name from the loaded dataset can be entered. The level of sophistication of the simulation increases as do the data requirements.

There are three types of input variables—categorical, binary, and continuous—and these can be defined at the individual or household level. In the **Main** tab, ADePT presents three groups of variables: **Main variables**, **Non-labor income components**, and **Education variables** (figure 4.11).

Figure 4.11: Main Form – Survey Variables

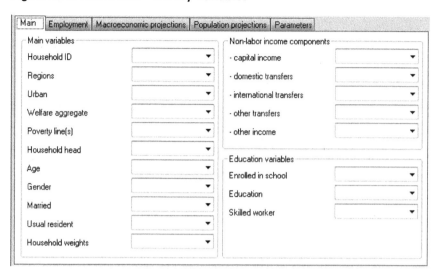

Table 4.15 provides some guidance on concepts behind these variables and how they can be built. Methodological problems and possible solutions, which are beyond the scope of this manual, are not discussed.

The definition of each labor market variable is country specific and varies depending on how information is collected in the labor force or household survey (table 4.16). As mentioned before, these are only guidelines to deal with some problems that may occur when processing the microdata.

Labor market information needed by the simulation is grouped in the **Employment** tab. This tab is divided into three subsets of data: **Labor force status**, **First job**, and **Second job** (figure 4.12). The labor force status set enables individuals within the working-age population who are "inactive or out of the labor force" to be distinguished from those who are active but "unemployed." The latter category (unemployed) must be chosen if the user wants to include it as part of the occupational choice model. Otherwise, the first category (**Out of labor force**) could include not only those workers who are inactive but also those who are unemployed, which could then be interpreted as non-employed workers. This last option is useful for those countries where unemployment is not a significant issue and does not warrant inclusion, or if there are not enough observations in the survey, which makes the occupational choice model almost impossible to converge.[13]

Table 4.15: List of Variables from Microdata - Main Tab

Field	Level	Type of variable	Concept
Main variables			
Household ID	Household	Continuous	Household identification variables that uniquely identify the household in the data.
Regions	Household	Categorical	Identifies each region within the country. For instance, in a country with four regions; the variable could be defined as 1 = South, 2 = North, 3 = East, and 4 = West.
Urban	Household	Binary	= 1 if the household is in an urban area.
Welfare aggregate	Household	Continuous	This variable depends on whether official poverty rates are estimated on consumption or income. Use the same unit of measure as the poverty line. For instance, if the poverty line is per capita per month then welfare measure must be per capita per month.
Poverty line(s)	Household	Continuous, constant, or binary indicators	One poverty line (a monetary value above which a household is not in poverty) corresponding to the selected welfare aggregate.
Household head	Individual	Binary	= 1 if the individual is the household head.
Age	Individual	Continuous	The individual's age in years.
Gender	Individual	Binary	The individual's gender (= 1 if male).
Married	Individual	Binary	The individual's marital status (= 1 if married).
Usual resident	Individual	Binary	Members of the main household; excludes servants or household employees. Equals 1 for usual resident.
Household weights	Household		Survey household weights. Equal for every household member and used to expand results to total population.
Non-labor income components			
- capital income	Household	Continuous	Includes all income from rentals, interest, and dividends from investments.
- domestic transfers	Household	Continuous	Total assistance received from domestic sources in cash and in kind.
- international transfers	Household	Continuous	Total assistance received from abroad in cash and in kind.
- other transfers	Household	Continuous	Includes pensions and retirement, social transfers, and other sources of income in cash or in kind.
- other income	Household	Continuous	Sum of other labor income from other jobs not classified as primary or secondary and other non-labor income not considered in previous concepts. This residual variable must be generated and imputed to the household head. To derive this variable, total family income could be used if it is available in the household survey.
Education variables			
Enrolled in school	Individual	Binary	= 1 if the individual is enrolled.
Education	Individual	Continuous or categorical variable	Identifies the maximum education level achieved by the individual, or maximum years of education. The variable will be considered continuous if it has more than 10 distinct numeric values.
Skilled worker	Individual	Binary	Identifies individuals in the working-age population who are skilled, based on education level. For instance, skilled includes the last three out of seven levels of education or individuals with more than nine years of education.

Table 4.16: List of Variables from Microdata - Employment Tab

Field	Level	Type of variable	Concept
Labor force status			
Out of labor force	Individual	Binary	= 1 if the individual is out of the labor force. This definition varies across countries and sometimes refers to a different reference period from that used for labor income. So, we suggest considering an individual to be out of the labor force if he or she has NO labor income and is NOT seeking a job.
Unemployed	Individual	Binary	= 1 if the individual is unemployed. This definition varies across countries and sometimes refers to a different reference period from that used for labor income. We suggest considering an individual to be unemployed if he or she has NO labor income and IS seeking a job.
First job			
– salaried	Individual	Binary	= 1 if the individual is a daily wage or salaried worker.
– self-employed	Individual	Binary	= 1 if the individual is self-employed (either with or without employees).
– unpaid workers	Individual	Binary	= 1 if the individual is an unpaid family worker
Sector	Individual	Categorical	Economic sector of main activity (agriculture, industry, or services). This must match the sector classification in the macro data.
Public sector	Individual	Binary	= 1 if the individual is employed in the public sector or in a state-owned enterprise.
Labor income	Individual	Continuous	Earnings from main occupation at the individual level. For the self-employed (with or without employees), the net revenue from agriculture or nonagriculture activities must be allocated to all household members who work in the family business, either per capita or by hours of work.
Second job			
- salaried	Individual	Binary	= 1 if the individual is a daily wage or salaried worker.
- self-employed	Individual	Binary	= 1 if the individual is self-employed (either with or without employees).
- unpaid workers	Individual	Binary	= 1 if the individual is an unpaid family worker.
Sector	Individual	Categorical	Economic sector of secondary activity (agriculture, industry, or services). This must match the sector classification in the macro data. If there is no information, sector from First job should be used.
Labor income	Individual	Continuous	Earnings from secondary occupation at the individual level.

It is important to take into account how the household or labor force survey collects the information about labor status and labor income. Sometimes the labor force status questions refer to a different reference period than the labor income questions. Thus, it is quite possible to have individuals who are defined as unemployed or inactive according to the first set of questions but have positive labor income. These inconsistencies must be resolved in advance. One option is to define individuals out of the labor force who have no labor income and who are not seeking a job and those who have no labor income and are seeking a job. In other words, labor market participation is income based, so a person is classified as employed if any labor income (wage or self-employment income) is recorded by the survey.[14]

The other inputs required for the simulation are for the **First job** and **Second job**. The first group of variables is related to whether the individual

Figure 4.12: Employment – Labor Force Status

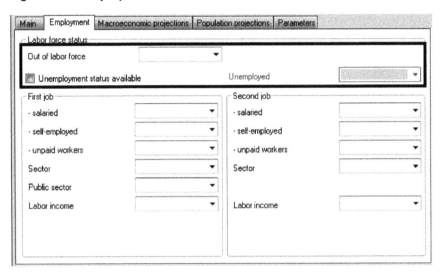

is salaried, self-employed (including workers with and without employees), or unpaid, (such as family workers).

The **Sector** field specifies the economic sector, such as agriculture, industry, or services, in which the individual works. This classification must be done in the same order in which the macro data has been classified. For instance, if macro projections are available for tradable and nontradable sectors, then microdata must be grouped similarly. The order is essential because it relates to the order followed by **Growth of sector GDP** in the **Macroeconomic projections** tab.

Individuals working in the public sector or at a state-owned enterprise are assumed to remain employed and their labor earnings are adjusted in line with adjustments to their sectors (agriculture, industry, or services). This option is considered in the simulation by including a binary variable equal to 1 for employment in the **Public sector** field. Similarly, for workers holding more than one job, the simulation assumes the employment sector of their secondary activity remains constant, and earnings are adjusted in line with sector change.[15]

Labor income for First job is an important variable that is used not only in the earning equations estimations but also throughout the simulation process. It is acknowledged that net revenues from farm and nonfarm businesses are allocated mostly to the household head or to the member running the family business. However, the simulation works at the individual level and complete information for each worker is necessary. Therefore, net revenues from agriculture or nonagriculture activities could be allocated to all household members who work in the family business. One possible option is to allocate this total amount on either a per capita basis or by hours of work.

Other Options

The ADePT Simulation Module enables the simulation to be tailored by choosing different options in the **Parameters** tab (figure 4.13). One of these options is the **Remittances allocation method: Simple** or **Random rank**. The simple approach only rescales the recipient households' amount up or down using the growth rate for international remittances in the Macroeconomic projections tab. The random rank method adds new recipient households when total remittances increase. It scales them down when total remittances decrease, keeping constant the number of recipient households.[16]

The **Adjust weights** option enables survey weights to be adjusted at either the individual or household level. In most household surveys, the household is the unit that is sampled and each household member has

Figure 4.13: Parameters

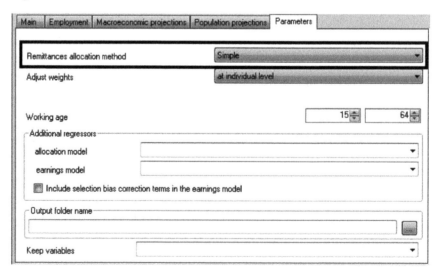

the same weight. If this is the case, survey weights must be adjusted at the household level.

The **Working age** of the population can also be redefined. By default, the interval covers individuals between 15 and 64 years old, but it can be changed by typing or clicking the arrows. Other control variables can be added to the **allocation model** and **earnings model** by typing their names separated by spaces. The **earnings model** can also be corrected by selecting the **Include selection bias correction terms in the earnings model** option.

It is important to fill in the **Output folder name** field, which specifies where the simulation's outputs will be saved. Note that the ADePT Simulation Module overwrites results when the simulation is run more than once. Be careful to change the folder's path if you run several alternative scenarios and want to compare these results afterward.

The **Keep variables** field is described in the "Output Datasets" section of chapter 5.

Notes

1. For information about installing ADePT software, see www.worldbank .org/adept.
2. For further explanation of how the module adjusts by population growth, see the "Populating Growth" section in chapter 2.
3. http://esa.un.org/unpd/wpp/unpp/panel_population.htm.
4. These could be interpreted as the linking aggregate variables (LAVs) in a top-down modeling approach. See Bourguignon, Bussolo. and Pereira da Silva (2008).
5. Some countries produce macroeconomic projections over the year based on a Macroeconomic model or CGE. The Benchmark scenario could be those projections that the country generates before those which include a macro-shock. Another source of information could be IMF WEO projections.
6. For further details about different macro models, see Bussolo et al. (2008); and Ferreira et al. (2008).
7. The user can at least create these relations based on two points in time. For Bangladesh, during the global financial crisis, Bilal et al. (2010) used the last available data, which was two points: 2000 and 2005.

8. The definition of total working-age population may vary by country. However, most countries define it as 15 years old and older.
9. For further details about the Mexican case, see World Bank (2010).
10. The activity rate is defined as the ratio of the labor force to the total population.
11. More-sophisticated econometric techniques can be used to calculate this elasticity.
12. This is not necessarily correct given that we are using the poverty line's basket, which is representative of the poor's consumption patterns instead of those of the population as a whole, but this is often the best approximation available.
13. Every category within each occupational choice model (that is, inactivity, unemployment, agriculture, industry, and services) must have enough observations to converge and find a solution. The simulation runs two occupational choice models for low-skill and high-skill workers with a minimum of four categories (non-employed, agriculture, industry, and services) and up to six labor categories (inactivity, unemployed, agriculture, manufacturing, other industries, and services).
14. It is important to note that this definition may affect those individuals who are nonpaid (family) workers and might be classified as inactive.
15. See the "Labor Income" section in the "Technical Discussion" chapter (chapter 2).
16. Further details about the random rank simulation are in the "International Remittances" section of chapter 2.

References

Bourguignon, F., M. Bussolo, and L. Pereira da Silva. 2008. "The Impact of Macroeconomic Policies on Poverty and Income Distribution: Macro-Micro Evaluation Techniques and Tools." In *The Impact of Macroeconomic Policies on Poverty and Income Distribution: Macro-Micro Evaluation Techniques and Tools*, edited by F. Bourguignon, M. Bussolo, and L. Pereira da Silva. Washington, DC: World Bank.

Bussolo, M., J. Lay, D. Medvedev, and D. van der Mensbrugghe. 2008. "Trade Options for Latin America: A Poverty Assessment Using a Top-Down Macro-Micro Modeling Framework." In *The Impact of*

Macroeconomic Policies on Poverty and Income Distribution: Macro-Micro Evaluation Techniques and Tools, edited by F. Bourguignon, M. Bussolo, and L. Pereira da Silva. Washington, DC: World Bank.

Ferreira, F., P. Leite, L. Pereira da Silva, and P. Picchetti. 2008. "Can the Distributional Impacts of Macroeconomic Shocks Be Predicted? A Comparison of Top-Down Macro-Micro Models with Historical Data for Brazil." In *The Impact of Macroeconomic Policies on Poverty and Income Distribution: Macro-Micro Evaluation Techniques and Tools*, edited by F. Bourguinon, M. Bussolo, and L. Pereira da Silva. Washington, DC: World Bank.

Habib, B., A. Narayan, S. Olivieri, and C. Sánchez-Páramo. 2010. "Assessing Poverty and Distributional Impacts of the Global Crisis in The Philippines: A Microsimulation Approach." Policy Research Working Paper 5286, World Bank, Washington, DC.

World Bank. 2010. "Recent Trends and Forecasts of Poverty in Mexico: A Poverty Note." Unpublished, Latin America and the Caribbean Region, World Bank, Washington, DC.

Chapter 5

Outputs

As mentioned in previous chapters, the ADePT Simulation Module is different from other ADePT modules[1] in its outputs and estimation complexity. It produces several key tables in the output report, mostly focusing on the performance of the simulation method. It also generates datasets—for each simulated scenario—that can be used as inputs in other ADePT modules (such as Poverty and Inequality), or processed in other statistical packages (such as Stata or SPSS, any versions) to perform further distributional analysis. These output datasets are saved in Stata format regardless of the input format used.

Tables

After loading all macro and micro inputs into the module, the user selects the tables to generate in the upper right panel of the ADePT window (figure 5.1). The tables that can be generated (that is, that are feasible) are displayed in black, while those that cannot be created are displayed in gray. Most tables generated by this module describe the simulation's accuracy in reaching the targets on employment allocation status, economic growth, and total time used for conducting the simulation. Some of these tables show the impacts of the simulated changes.

The three **Diagnostic tables** include estimated results of the occupational choice and earning models and the simulated occupation status. The first two models are calculated for two types of workers classified by their skill level

Figure 5.1: ADePT Simulation Module Tables

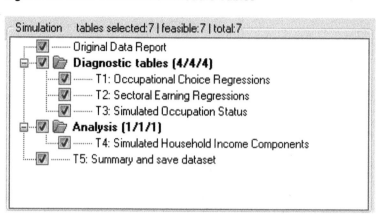

(low and high) within the defined working-age range (generally between 15 and 64 years old). Estimation results of the occupational choice model are presented in output worksheet *T1: Occupational Choice Regressions*. The dependent variable could have four or five categories: non-employed and three economic sectors such as agriculture, industry, and services, with the first category (non-employed) as a reference.

The set of explanatory variables includes not only individuals' but also households' characteristics. These characteristics are standard covariates such as education level, gender, dependency ratio, marital status, region, and area, among others. Other variables can also be selected in the **Parameters** tab (figure 4.13). All coefficients are differences with respect to the base category, and their magnitudes are difficult to interpret. However, their signs and significance levels are important and must be considered when further analyzing simulation results. For example, suppose a dependent variable has four categories: non-employed, agriculture, industry, and services, with non-employed as the base category. Assume also that all coefficients for the binary variable that identifies the household head are positive for all sectoral categories. In other words, being a head of household increases the probability of being employed in an economic sector relative to being non-employed.[2]

Estimation results of the Mincerian log earning equations are presented in output worksheet *T2: Sectoral Earning Regressions*.[3] The sample used for these estimations includes all employed workers in an economic sector with positive labor income within the defined working-age population. The module runs two sets of regressions according to worker skill level (low and high skill). A maximum of eight regressions result when considering a maximum of four economic sectors such as agriculture, manufacturing, other industries, and services. The number of sectors corresponds to those chosen and are similar to those considered in the occupational choice model. The dependent variable is the logarithm of the main labor income, and the control variables are standards such as age, gender, level of education, and relationship with household head, among others. The set of explanatory variables can also be expanded in the **Parameters** tab. Interpretation of these coefficients is straightforward. For instance, assume a positive coefficient for years of education (β_{ed}). Multiplying this coefficient by 100 (%Δearnings $\cong$ ($\beta_{ed} \times 100$)Δyears of education) yields the percentage change in earnings given one additional year of education, keeping all else constant (Wooldridge 2002).

The *Simulated Occupation Status* is shown in worksheet *T3* of the output report (table 5.1). This table presents the main occupational status in percentage terms. The unemployment and the employment rates are calculated including *all individuals* in or out the working-age population. It also shows

Table 5.1: Simulated Occupation Status

	SIM1
Proportions	
lab_rel == 4 (Unemployed)	
_UNEMP_SIM1_0000	95.50
_UNEMP_SIM1_0001	4.50
occupation category	
_OCCUPATION_SIM1_0000	34.76
_OCCUPATION_SIM1_0001	2.83
_OCCUPATION_SIM1_0002	7.63
_OCCUPATION_SIM1_0003	10.45
_OCCUPATION_SIM1_0004	5.76
_OCCUPATION_SIM1_0005	38.57
labor force in the sample	
_LF_SAMPLE_SIM1_0000	34.76
_LF_SAMPLE_SIM1_0001	65.24
Employed	
_EMPLOYED_SIM1_0000	58.09
_EMPLOYED_SIM1_0001	41.91

the labor force participation and occupation shares considering only the working-age population. All of these proportions are calculated for each simulated scenario, and it is easy to compare how the occupation structure changes between them. For instance, more than third of the working-age population is inactive (_OCCUPATION_SIM1_0000). From those who are active about 3 percent are unemployed (_OCCUPATION_SIM1_0001), 8 percent are employed in agriculture (_OCCUPATION_SIM1_0002), 10 percent in manufacturing (_OCCUPATION_SIM1_0003), 6 percent in other industries (_OCCUPATION_SIM1_0004), and 39 percent in services (_OCCUPATION_SIM1_0005).

The income structure table, presented in worksheet *T4*, shows what proportion of the total household income is contributed by its major components: *labor* and *non-labor* income. It presents averages and shares for each simulated scenario at the per capita and income-receiving-household levels. It also reports the contribution of other non-labor income components: rents, dividends, and other capital assets, and domestic and international transfers. This table is in worksheet *T4: Simulated Household Income Components* of the output report. For instance, the average total per capita income is about $2,811 in the first simulated scenario and almost 84 percent comes from labor economic activities undertaken by different household members (table 5.2).

The third column reports averages based on households with positive labor or non-labor income components. In this example, there is not much difference between mean per capita and mean per receiving household for

Table 5.2: Income Structure

	Overall mean per capita (1)	Overall share (2)	Mean per income-receiving household (3)	Percent receiving (4) [(1)/(3)]
Simulation scenario 1				
Total income	2,810.93	100.00	2,810.93	100.00
Labor income	2,352.69	83.70	2,452.75	95.92
Non-labor income	458.24	16.30	910.50	50.33
Capital income	65.79	1.97	1,269.22	5.18
Domestic transfers	0.00	0.00	0.00	0.00
Transfers from abroad	49.20	1.48	1,014.38	4.85
Simulation scenario 2				
Total income	2,381.14	100.00	2,399.77	100.00
Labor income	1,924.92	80.84	2,041.48	94.29
Non-labor income	456.22	19.16	907.72	50.26
Capital income	54.78	1.96	1,049.60	5.22
Domestic transfers	0.00	0.00	0.00	0.00
Transfers from abroad	49.37	1.76	1,006.83	4.90

the total income and labor income components in scenario 1. However, significant differences arise when considering total non-labor income and its components. For instance, the mean for transfers from abroad jumps from $49 per capita to $1,014 per receiving household in scenario 1, showing that the first number is not indicative of the average transfer amount received by households. This could also indicate that the majority of households do not receive or do not report positive transfers from abroad. The last column presents the ratio of mean per capita income components to the mean of receiving households.

Finally, the module offers two unclassified tables as Excel output tables: *Original Data Report* and *Summary and save dataset*. The first table presents information about variables selected for the analysis, such as the number of observations with nonmissing values, mean, minimum, maximum, percentiles, and the number of unique values. The second table shows how well the estimation process fits the targets or macroeconomic inputs specified for each scenario. It presents the total population, employment, and income growth rates, and proportions or shares for targets and simulated scenarios by occupation category (that is, active, inactive, unemployed, and economic sector). This option must be selected to obtain the output dataset files described in the next section.

Table 5.3 presents the results, by economic sector, of simulating an increase of only 10 percent of total GDP.[4] The table shows no change in population, employment growth targets, and shares. As expected, the only changes occur in the income dimension. Simulated growth rates are almost identical to the targets.

Output Datasets

The main outputs of the ADePT Simulation Module are different datasets that can then be used to perform further poverty, inequality, and employment analysis using complementary ADePT modules and other statistical packages. To obtain these datasets, select *Summary and save dataset* in the module's output options. The number of datasets generated depends on the number of scenarios considered in the simulation. The minimum number results when neither a treatment or second scenario is specified. In this case the module produces three datasets: ORIGINAL, ALL, and SCENARIO1, saved in Stata format.

Each dataset includes different variables that can be grouped in three sets: those not used in the simulation (Group 1), those used but not changed (Group 2), and those used and changed in the simulation (Group 3). Table 5.4 presents an example of how a few variables are classified in each group.

The ALL dataset includes variables from all variables' sets: used, not used, changed, or not changed in the simulation. Simulated variables can be easily identified by their labels or names, which end with _SIM1 or _SIM2,

Table 5.3: Summary and Save Dataset

	Active	Inactive	Unemployed	Agriculture	Manufacturing	Other industries	Services
Population at baseline	44836080.0	23730130.0	1929360.0	5300950.0	7271650.0	3939600.0	26394520.0
Population in Scenario 1	44836080.0	23730130.0	1929360.0	5300950.0	7271650.0	3939600.0	26394520.0
Simulated employment growth, Scenario 1	0.0		0.0	0.0	0.0	0.0	0.0
Employment growth target, Scenario 1	0.0		0.0	0.0	0.0	0.0	0.0
Simulated income growth, Scenario 1				0.10034	0.099975	0.099975	0.099975
Income growth target, Scenario 1				0.1	0.1	0.1	0.1
Population proportions at baseline	0.653909	0.346091	0.043031	0.123546	0.169476	0.091818	0.615161
Population proportions in Scenario 1	0.653909	0.346091	0.043031	0.123546	0.169476	0.091818	0.615161

Table 5.4: Classification of an Example List of Variables

	Not changed	Changed
Not used	Anthropometric variables Expenditure components Micro credit variables Safety net programs and the like	not applicable
Used	Household ID Region Area Household head Age Gender Married Enrolled in school Education level	Labor force status Salaried worker Unemployed Employed Sector of employment main activity Transfers from abroad Labor income first job Labor income second job Weights

for Scenario 1 and Scenario 2, respectively. All not-used variables remain unchanged while variables in Group 2 are checked for consistency by the module.[5] The module corrects as few variables as possible, and displays messages about changes in the lower right corner of the ADePT window. All variables used in the simulation are labeled and named with an underscore (_) and capital letters.

Having all variables in the same dataset makes it easy to compare different population groups. For instance, it is very easy to identify individuals whose occupational or poverty status has been changed by the simulation. However, if population changes are included in the simulation, they must be taken into account by using proper weights when comparing original and simulated variables. In other words, original variables must be weighted by original weights (_WEIGHTS) while simulated variables must be weighted by their respective simulated weights (_WEIGHTS_SIM#). This dataset also includes additional variables that describe the poverty status of individuals before (for example, _THE_POOR_0) and after (for example, _THE_POOR_SIM#) the simulation, as well as those who change poverty status in either way: from poor to non-poor (_FROM_POOR_SIM#) and from non-poor to poor (_TO_POOR_SIM#).

The simulated datasets (SCENARIO#.dta) include by default all variables used in the simulation. This means that these variables come from the changed and not-changed sets (Groups 2 and 3) and keep the names of the ORIGINAL dataset. Keeping the names of the original dataset allows the use of other ADePT modules. For example, in the Poverty Module, more than one dataset can be included (for instance, ORIGINAL and SCENARIO1) to quickly produce a Poverty report that could include not only poverty levels for each dataset but also differences between them. Variables' labels help to distinguish variables of the changed set (simulated) from those of the not-changed set (retained). To take advantage of this option, the **Keep variables** option must be selected to include additional variables from Group 1 in the simulated databases. This option is located at the bottom of the **Parameters** tab (figure 5.2).

Starting from the Outputs: Further Analysis

One advantage of using this simulation process is the possibility of fully taking into account the heterogeneity of individuals observed in the

Figure 5.2: Keep Variables Option

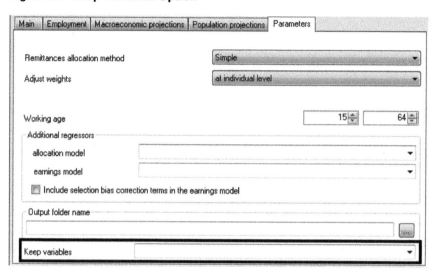

household survey. Individuals likely to be winners or losers from the predicted macroeconomic change can be identified with some precision. There are many ways to exploit the simulated datasets. For example, the "new poor" could be profiled or those who would become unemployed as a consequence of the macro or policy change could be identified, among other possibilities.

We want to emphasize that micro-simulation outputs (that is, original and simulated datasets) could be used as a starting point to predict the potential impact of policy responses, allowing questions such as the following to be answered:

- How would automatic stabilizers (such as unemployment benefits) work after the economy has been hit by a macro shock?
- How would an expansion of a specific program help those in need?
- How much would these measures cost if some parameters of the program were to be changed—for example, by increasing the amount transferred by the program or by changing the age limit of those eligible for it?

We present two examples of simulations conducted for Poland and Mexico, focusing in both cases on the impact of an increase in social assistance on poverty (for further details, see Habib et al. 2012). During the

2008–09 financial crisis, Poland suffered a combination of lower employment levels and lower earnings, which translated into lower household labor income. However, non-labor income increased, mainly due to unemployment insurance benefits. This benefit was administered according to precrisis rules, and its increase offset some of the losses in labor income. As a result, the poverty headcount rate was projected to increase less than without this automatic stabilizer (Habib et al. 2012). The distribution of the benefit across deciles showed that a large share of the total amount expended was concentrated in the middle-top of the distribution, protecting them from declining income as a consequence of the crisis (figure 5.3). However, the incidence of the benefit was mainly concentrated at the bottom of the distribution.

To simulate the impact of a government's crisis response package, such as a family allowance, an increase of 20 percent in these transfers is computed. This projected increase in social transfers would further reduce the poverty headcount ratio. Figure 5.4 shows that this additional amount would primarily be located at the lower deciles.

Figure 5.3: Policy Response Simulation: Unemployment Insurance

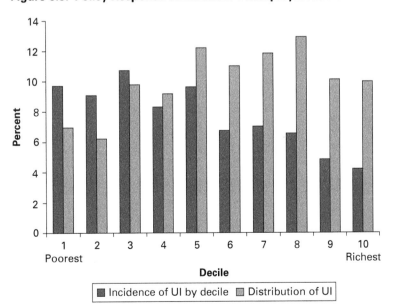

Source: Estimations based on data from Habib et al. 2012.
Note: UI = unemployment insurance.

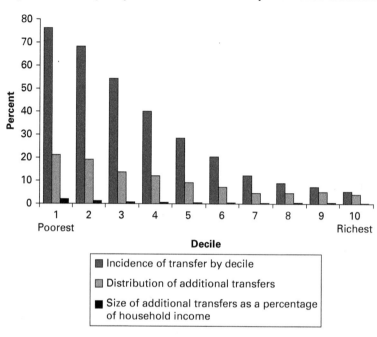

Figure 5.4: Policy Response Simulation: Family Allowance Transfers

Source: Estimations based on data from Habib et al. 2012.

In Mexico, the expansion of existing safety net programs—Oportunidades and the Nutrition Assistance Program (Programa de Apoyo Alimentario, or PAL)—was simulated to increase the number of beneficiaries by 1 million.[6] The simulations considered two different extreme hypothetical targeting scenarios based on existing targeting methods in the country. Scenario 1 assumes perfect targeting of the poorest, that is, that new beneficiary households would be those with the lowest welfare score nationally (among nonbeneficiary households).[7] Scenario 2 assumes that new beneficiary households would be chosen from poor households that are closest to the poverty line nationally. Neither of these extreme scenarios would reflect the actual targeting strategy used by the government, but they are useful in providing upper and lower bounds on poverty impacts.

As expected, Scenario 1 had a greater impact on the "always poor,"[8] who benefit the most from the proposed expansion. However, the poverty head-count rate is not projected to decline. On the one hand, 1 million additional beneficiaries represents a large expansion with respect to existing coverage, but it is only 2 percent of the projected number of moderate poor. On the other hand, these new beneficiaries are so far below the moderate and even extreme poverty lines that the amount of the transfer would not be sufficient to pull them out of poverty.

Despite the lack of impact on poverty headcount, the transfer is likely to have a significant impact on the livelihoods of new beneficiary households. For instance, the average simulated Oportunidades transfer represents 19 percent of total household income and 115 percent of per capita pretransfer household income of new beneficiaries. To illustrate this point further, the cumulative density function of per capita income among new beneficiary households before and after the simulated expansion of the programs is shown in figure 5.5. The cumulative density function shifts to the right after the expansion, and final distribution dominates the initial one.

The impact is larger on depth and severity of poverty because the transfers would reduce the new beneficiaries' distance from both poverty lines. On the other extreme, Scenario 2 would result in a higher impact on the

Figure 5.5: Cumulative Density Function of per Capita Income among New Beneficiary Households
(before and after expansion of Oportunidades and PAL)

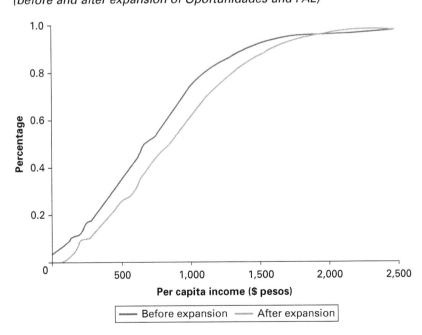

Source: World Bank 2010.

poverty headcount than would Scenario 1, but a lower impact on the depth and severity of poverty.

Regardless of whether the actual expansion was closer to one or the other scenario, new beneficiary households are much more likely to be chosen from among the "always poor" than from among other groups (the "new poor" and the non-poor). This is consistent with the official program goal of serving the extreme and chronic poor.

Notes

1. ADePT software is a free download available at www.worldbank.org/adept.
2. For further discussions about how to interpret these coefficients, see chapter 15 of Wooldridge (2002).
3. The ADePT Simulation Module uses the natural logarithm.
4. See exercise 1 under "Simulating Changes in Total and Sector GDP" in chapter 7.
5. ADePT Simulation makes consistency checks according to the way variables should be defined as explained in table 4.15.
6. For additional details on methodological aspects of the expansion of the programs, see World Bank (2010) and Habib et al. (2012).
7. The proxy means test formula of the Social Transfer Program used.
8. The "always poor" can be understood to be either those who were poor before the crisis and remained so, or those who were poor after the crisis and have a low probability of exiting poverty by 2011. For further details of the simulation exercise, see World Bank (2010).

References

Habib, B., A. Narayan, S. Olivieri, and C. Sánchez-Páramo. 2012. "Assessing the Poverty and Distributional Impacts of the Financial Crisis with Microsimulations: An Overview of Country Studies." In *Knowing, When You Do Not Know. Simulating the Poverty and Distributional Impacts of an Economic Crisis*, edited by A. Narayan and C. Sánchez-Páramo. Washington, DC: World Bank.

Wooldridge, J. 2002. *Econometric Analysis of Cross Section and Panel Data.* Cambridge, Massachusetts: MIT Press.

World Bank. 2010. "Recent Trends and Forecasts of Poverty in Mexico: A Poverty Note." Unpublished, Latin America and the Caribbean Region, World Bank, Washington, DC.

Chapter 6

Condensed Instructions

These instructions summarize the discussion presented in chapter 4. Section titles and page numbers for each step point to the corresponding details.

Step	Section containing details	Page
1. Prepare the following data for baseline and projected years:		
a. Macroeconomic projection data	Generating Total and Sector Changes in Employment and Labor Force Participation Data	51
b. (Optional) Population growth data	Generating Population Growth Rate Data	45
c. (Optional) Estimated employment-output elasticity by economic sector and activity-output elasticity	Estimating Employment-Output Elasticity by Economic Sector and Estimating Activity-Output Elasticity	52
d. Growth rates of activity, unemployment, and employment, total and by sector	Generating Employment Data	58
e. Changes in macroeconomic remittances from abroad	Generating Data on Changes in Remittances from Abroad	60
f. Change in poverty line	Generating and Entering Price Data	62
2. Launch ADePT and select the Simulation module.	ADePT documentation (http://go.worldbank.org/1HHHLLELG0)	—
3. In ADePT's upper left panel, specify datasets.	ADePT documentation (see link above)	—
The following steps take place in ADePT's lower left panel.		
1. In the **Main** tab, make selections in the **Main variables**, **Non-labor income components**, and **Education variables** panels.	Microeconomic Inputs	64
2. In the **Employment** tab, make selections in the **Labor force status**, **First job**, and **Second job** panels.	Microeconomic Inputs	64
3. In the **Macroeconomic projections** tab:		
a. To compare two scenarios, activate the **Specify second scenario** option.	Entering Growth-of-Sector-GDP Data	48
b. Just below the **Specify scenario model** option, select **3-sector model** or **4-sector model**.	Entering Growth-of-Sector-GDP Data	48

(continued)

(continued)

Step	Section containing details	Page
c. In the **Employment growth** columns, enter employment growth rate data* for **Scenario 1** (and **Scenario 2**, if that option has been selected).	Entering Employment Data	59
d. In the **Growth of sector GDP** columns, enter sector GDP growth rate data* for **Scenario 1** (and **Scenario 2**, if that option has been selected).	Entering Growth-of-Sector-GDP Data	48
e. In the **Growth** panel:		
i. For **Sectoral employment growth rates**, select either **Relative (growth of shares)** or **Absolute (growth of # of workers)**, as desired.	—	
ii. If **Sectoral employment growth rates** is set to **Relative (growth of shares)**, then in the **in labor active population, overall** row, enter labor active population growth rates* for **Scenario 1** (and **Scenario 2**, if that option has been selected).	Entering Employment Data	59
iii. In the **in unemployment** row, enter unemployment growth rate data* in **Scenario 1** (and **Scenario 2**, if that option has been selected).	Entering Employment Data	59
iv. In the **of total GDP** row, enter labor income growth rate data* for **Scenario 1** (and **Scenario 2**, if that option has been selected).	Entering Growth-of-Sector-GDP Data	48
v. In the **in poverty line** row, enter poverty line growth rate data* for **Scenario 1** (and **Scenario 2**, if that option has been selected).	Generating and Entering Price Data	62
vi. In the **in remittances from abroad** row, enter remittances data* for **Scenario 1** (and **Scenario 2**, if that option has been selected).	Entering Data on Changes in Remittances from Abroad	62
4. In the **Population projections** tab:		
a. Set the **From** and **To** ages, set the **Interval** (that is, how many years in each age group), then click the **Set** button.	Entering Population Growth Rate Data	45
b. Enter the population growth rates in the **Males** and **Females** columns of the grid.	Entering Population Growth Rate Data	45
5. In the **Parameters** tab:		
a. Select the **Remittances allocation method**.	Other Options	70
b. Select the **Adjust weights** option.	Other Options	70
c. Set the lower and upper limits of the **Working age**.	Other Options	70
d. Add other control variables to the **allocation model** (optional).	Other Options	70
e. Add other control variables to the **earnings model** (optional).	Other Options	70
f. As needed, activate **Include selection bias correction terms in the earnings model**.	Other Options	70
g. Specify the **Output folder name** where the simulation results will be generated.	Other Options	70
The following step takes place in ADePT's upper right panel.		
1. Select the desired output tables and datasets.	Tables (chapter 5)	75
2. Select the desired output datasets.	Output Datasets (chapter 5)	79
3. Click the **Generate** button.		

Note: *Data should be entered as decimals, not percentages.

Chapter 7

Exercises

This chapter presents a set of exercises based on a sample of the 2008 Mexico Household Survey. Each exercise tries different combinations of assumptions to show how each part of the micro-simulation model works independently. For instance, all exercises in "Simulating Changes in Total and Sector GDP" are focused on how changes in total GDP and economic sector GDP affect poverty, assuming there are no changes in employment, prices, population, or international remittances. The main output indicator shown in this problem set is the headcount poverty rate. The solution for the first exercise of each set is shown; correction for selection bias is not chosen.

Simulating Changes in Total and Sector GDP

Assume there is no population growth; total and economic sector employment rates are inelastic to changes in GDP; there are no changes in prices of food and non-food; and there are no changes in international remittances. Under these assumptions:

1. Simulate an increase of 10 percent in total real GDP with equal growth rates in each economic sector (Input 1 row of table 7.1). Does the headcount poverty rate increase? Does the income distribution change?

2. Simulate a growth rate of 10 percent in total real GDP as a consequence of an 25 percent increase in manufacturing and an 9 percent

increase in services (Input 2 row of table 7.1). How does the poverty headcount rate vary compared with the first exercise?

3. Simulate an increase in services of 3 percent, which is offset by a decrease in manufacturing of 10 percent (Input 3 row of table 7.1). In other words, there is no movement in total real GDP. Is there any change in the poverty headcount rate?

4. Simulate a decrease of 10 percent in total real GDP as result of an increase of 1 percent in manufacturing and reductions of 7 percent and 15 percent in agriculture and services, respectively (Input row 4 of table 7.1). What happens to poverty rates? How about poverty headcount rates by urban and rural areas?

Simulating Changes in Employment

Assume there is no population growth; total and economic sector employment rates are inelastic to changes in GDP; there are no changes in prices of food and non-food; and there are no changes in international remittances. Simulate the following shifts of employed individuals between economic sectors and status. All growth rates are calculated based on changes in shares.

1. Simulate a reduction of 10 percent in employment in agriculture and manufacturing with an increase of 4.5 percent in employment in services and no changes in other industries. The activity and unemployment rates remain constant. Does the headcount poverty rate increase? Is there a change in the income distribution?

2. Simulate decreases in employment of 11.05 percent and 4.98 percent in manufacturing and other industries, respectively; and increases in employment of 11.18 percent in agriculture and 1.08 percent in services. This shift between sectors raises the unemployment rate 21.5 percent and produces no changes in the activity rate. How does the poverty headcount rate vary by area?

Simulating Changes in the Poverty Line

Assume there is no population growth; total and economic sector employment rates are inelastic to changes in GDP; and there are no changes in international remittances. The poverty line in the country is expressed in prices of one specific region. The shares of the food and non-food baskets in the poverty line are 49.8 percent and 50.2 percent, respectively. The share of the food basket in the consumer price index (CPI) is 23 percent and the rest refers to the non-food basket. Under these assumptions and information about the poverty line and CPI structures:

1. Simulate an increase in both food and non-food prices of 7.4 percent and 4.5 percent, respectively. How much does the poverty line change? What happens to the national poverty rate?
2. Simulate a 4.5 percent decrease in non-food prices and an increase of 25 percent in food prices. How much does the poverty line change? Does the headcount poverty rate increase?

Simulating Changes in International Remittances

Under the assumptions of no population growth; total and economic sector employment rates that are inelastic to changes in GDP; and no changes in prices of food and non-food:

1. Simulate an increase in international remittances of 10 percent in nominal terms in foreign currency units and a constant exchange rate. How much do international remittances change in real terms? Does the headcount poverty rate decrease?
2. Simulate an increase in international remittances of 10 percent in nominal terms in foreign currency units and a decrease of 18 percent in the exchange rate. How much do international remittances change in real terms? Is there a change in the headcount poverty rate?

Simulating Changes in Population

Assume the total and economic sector employment rates are inelastic to changes in GDP; and there are no changes in prices of food and non-food or in international remittances:

1. Simulate a 20 percent increase in the female population between 20 and 60 years old for each age interval. Age intervals are defined as

10-year spans of a total population age range between 0 and 85 years old. Does the headcount poverty rate change?

2. Repeat exercise 1, but with a 10 percent decrease for each age bracket in the male population between 20 and 60 years old. Does the headcount poverty rate remain constant? How much does it vary compared with the results of the previous exercise?

Simulating Combined Changes in GDP and Labor Market Status

Assumptions are no population growth; no changes in prices of food and non-food or in international remittances; and the following employment-output elasticities apply: activity rate = −0.01; agriculture = −0.7; manufacturing = 0.1; other industries = 0.6; and services = 0.8. Inactivity and unemployment are the residual categories.

Tables 7.1 and 7.2 show the inputs for four potential exercises by combining their inputs. To estimate the results for the first exercise, the user must simultaneously use Input 1 of GDP growth rates (table 7.1) and Input 1 of Labor Force and Employment Structure (table 7.2), and so on.

Solutions

Simulating Changes in Total and Sector GDP

Even though the first element of the exercise clearly specifies the inputs necessary to run the simulation, it would be helpful to remind the user of how to generate the inputs based on raw data. The data requirements for this exercise are two: the first is total output and output by economic sector in at least two periods and for each scenario. This information must be expressed in real terms. The second requirement is the calculation of growth rates between the baseline and projected year.

Table 7.1 presents the information necessary to generate these inputs for the simulation. The first row of table 7.1 shows total and sectoral GDP for Mexico for 2008, and the second row of table 7.1 displays macroeconomic projections for a future year (based on Input 1). This information is in real

Table 7.1: GDP in Real Terms

	TOTAL	Agriculture	Manufacturing	Other industries	Services
2008	8,475,564	325,667	1,550,343	1,141,731	5,457,823
		358,234	1,705,378	1,255,904	6,003,605
Input 1	0.10	0.10	0.10	0.10	0.10
	9,323,121	325,667	1,933,985	1,141,731	5,921,737
Input 2	0.10	0.00	0.25	0.00	0.09
	8,475,564	325,667	1,401,633	1,141,731	5,606,533
Input 3	0.00	0.00	−0.10	0.00	0.03
	7,628,008	302,871	1,565,847	1,141,731	4,617,559
Input 4	−0.10	−0.07	0.01	0.00	−0.15

Table 7.2: Labor Force and Employment Structure
(Estimations based on GDP growth rates and output-employment elasticity)

Unit	Total population	Inactive	Active	Unemployment	Employment TOTAL	Agriculture	Manufacturing	Other industries	Services
2008									
Millions	77.24	31.92	45.32	2.14	43.18	5.65	6.46	4.16	26.92
Percent		41.32	58.68	4.71	95.29	13.08	14.95	9.64	62.33
Elasticity			−0.01			−0.7	0.1	0.6	0.8
Millions	77.24	31.96	45.27	0.02	45.26	5.25	6.52	4.41	29.07
Percent		41.38	58.62	0.04	99.96	12.16	15.10	10.22	67.31
Input 1		0.0014	−0.0010	−0.9916	0.0490	−0.0700	0.0100	0.0600	0.0800
Millions	77.24	32.01	45.23	0.05	45.17	5.65	6.62	4.16	28.75
Percent		41.44	58.56	0.12	99.88	12.50	14.65	9.22	63.63
Input 2		0.0028	−0.0020	−0.9742	0.0482	−0.0441	−0.0204	−0.0441	0.0210
Millions	77.24	31.92	45.32	1.61	43.71	5.65	6.40	4.16	27.50
Percent		41.32	58.68	3.55	96.45	12.92	14.63	9.52	62.92
Input 3		0.00	0.00	−0.2457	0.0122	−0.0120	−0.0215	−0.0120	0.0095
Millions	77.24	31.87	45.36	5.21	40.15	5.92	6.46	4.16	23.60
Percent		41.26	58.74	11.49	88.51	14.76	16.10	10.37	58.78
Input 4		−0.0014	0.0010	1.4385	−0.0711	0.1282	0.0766	0.0755	−0.0570

terms and the baseline year is 2008. Each growth rate is calculated according to equations (7.1) and (7.2):

$$\Delta GDP_{t1-t0}^{T} = \frac{GDP_{t1}^{T} - GDP_{t0}^{T}}{GDP_{t0}^{T}} \text{ for total GDP} \qquad (7.1)$$

$$\Delta GDP_{t1-t0}^{s} = \frac{GDP_{t1}^{s} - GDP_{t0}^{s}}{GDP_{t0}^{s}} \text{ for each } s = 1,..,S \qquad (7.2)$$

for each economic sector.

The overall headcount poverty rate declines by 3.6 percentage points between the baseline and the projected year as consequence of a 10 percent increase of growth of the economy as a whole and in each economic sector. It is simple to imagine this poverty decrease by a shift to the right of the distribution curve (growth), with almost no changes in its shape (distribution) and no change in the poverty line as a consequence of no changes in relative prices (figure 7.1).

Simulating Changes in Employment

As in the previous exercise, the method for generating growth rates of employment shares is briefly reviewed. The starting point is actual information about the labor market structure for the baseline year. Table 7.3 shows that more than half of the employed working-age population is in services in Mexico and less than 5 percent of the total active population is unemployed.

The sectoral shift is simulated maintaining constant over time the total working-age population as well as the activity and unemployment rates. In other words, workers from agriculture and manufacturing are switching to services. For instance, workers may have temporary jobs in services because of seasonality.

Figure 7.1: Cumulative Distribution Function before and after Simulation

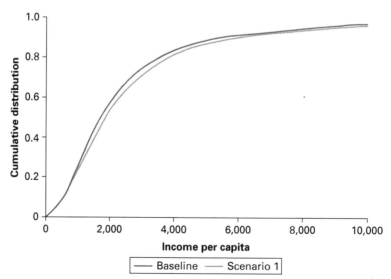

Table 7.3: Creating the Employment Input

	Unit	Total population	Inactive	Active	Unemployment	Employment				
						TOTAL	Agriculture	Manufacturing	Other industries	Services
2008										
	Millions	77.24	31.92	45.32	2.14	43.18	5.65	6.46	4.16	26.92
	Percent		41.3	58.7	4.7	95.3	13.1	15.0	9.6	62.3
Exercise 1										
	Millions	77.24	31.92	45.32	2.14	43.18	5.08	5.81	4.16	28.13
	Percent		41.3	58.7	4.7	95.3	11.8	13.5	9.6	65.1
	Input	0.0	0.0		0.0	0.0	−0.10	−0.10	0.0	0.04
Exercise 2										
	Millions	77.24	31.92	45.32	2.60	42.72	6.21	5.68	3.91	26.92
	Percent		41.3	58.7	5.73	94.27	14.5	13.3	9.2	63.0
	Input	0.0	0.0		0.2153	−0.0107	0.1118	−0.1105	−0.0498	0.0108

Table 7.4: Impacts of Changes in Employment Structure on Incidence of Poverty

	Poverty headcount rate		
	Actual	Projected	Change
Urban	43.7	43.8	0.1
Rural	54.8	55.1	0.3
Total	47.6	47.8	0.2

This intersectoral shift of workers produced an increase in the headcount poverty rate of less than 1 percentage point, mainly concentrated in rural areas where the headcount poverty rate increases 0.3 percentage point (table 7.4). One possible interpretation could be that these new entrants may be less qualified and are willing to work for lower wages. This would increase the competition for jobs and pull down the earnings of similar workers within this sector (under the assumption of no change in services GDP).

This simulation impacts the shape of the distribution curve rather than shifting the welfare distribution. To illustrate this point further, the Datt-Ravallion (1992) decomposition is computed. This decomposition splits the change in poverty into distribution-neutral growth, a redistributive effect, and a residual interpreted as an interaction term. As expected, the redistribution component explains almost all of the simulated increase in poverty (figure 7.2).

Figure 7.2: Growth and Redistribution Impacts by Area

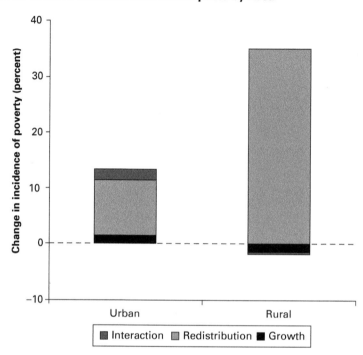

Simulating Changes in the Poverty Line

The following data are necessary to estimate changes in the poverty line: inflation rate projections (total, food, and non-food) as well as the shares of these baskets in the consumer price index (CPI) and the poverty line. Next, the total CPI has to be calculated as the weighted sum of food and non-food inflation. Shares of the CPI baskets are necessary in this step. Third, we use equation (4.16) from the "Generating and Entering Price Data" section of chapter 4 to calculate the growth rate of the poverty line. See table 7.5.

The result for the first exercise shows that an increase of 7.4 percent and 4.5 percent for food and non-food generates general inflation of 5.2 percent between the baseline and projected years. This produces a slight increase (less than 1 percentage point) in the poverty line as a consequence of a nonsignificant difference between food and non-food inflation rates. All in all, it is not surprising that the headcount poverty rate increases by a very small amount, less than one-half percentage point (table 7.6).

Table 7.5: Creating the Poverty Line Input

	Consumer price index			Adjustment in poverty line {[(2) × (6) + (3) × (7)]/ (1)} − 1
	General (1)	Food (2)	Non-Food (3)	
2008	100.0	100.0	100.0	
Exercise 1	105.2	107.4	104.5	0.0074
Exercise 2	102.3	125.0	95.5	0.0773
Share of food in consumer price index	23.0% (4)		Share of food in poverty line	49.8% (6)
Share of non-food in consumer price index	77.0% (5)		Share of non-food in poverty line	50.2% (7)

Table 7.6: Impacts of Changes in Poverty Line on Incidence of Poverty

	Poverty headcount rate		
	Actual	Projected	Change
Urban	43.7	44.0	0.3
Rural	54.8	55.3	0.5
Total	47.6	48.0	0.4

Simulating Changes in International Remittances

To estimate the total variation in international remittances between the baseline and projected years, it is necessary to express remittances in local currency unit real terms. Under the assumption of no inflation and a constant exchange rate over time, the variation of remittances in nominal and real terms yields a positive change of total remittances of 10 percent between the baseline and projected years (table 7.7).

Assuming a simple distribution of the additional amount of remittances, the headcount poverty rate decreases less than 1 percentage point. An impact is observed only on rural areas. This impact depends on the spatial distribution of remittances in the country and on the initial poverty status of the remittances-recipient households (table 7.8).

Simulating Changes in Population

The increase in the female working-age population affects the labor market for all workers. This change in population first affects labor market shares,

Table 7.7: Creating International Remittances Input

	R^N (1)	ε (2)	Consumer price index (3)	R^R [(1) × (2)]/(3)
2008	120	0.30	1	36.0
Exercise 1	132	0.30	1	39.6
Change	0.10	0.00	0.00	0.10
Exercise 2	132	0.25	1	32.5
Change	0.10	−0.18	0.00	−0.10

Table 7.8: Impacts of Changes in International Remittances on Incidence of Poverty

	Poverty headcount rate		
	Actual	Projected	Change
Urban	43.7	43.7	0.0
Rural	54.8	54.5	−0.2
Total	47.6	47.5	−0.1

with more female workers in services. However, the assumption for this exercise is no relative change in the labor market; thus, workers must be reallocated to keep labor market shares constant. This shift means that some employed individuals become unemployed and others switch sectors (figure 7.3).

These changes in the labor composition of the working-age population affect the labor income of workers through employment, labor income, or a combination of the two. First, some individuals become unemployed because of this population shift and now have zero labor income. Second, most workers receive less under this exercise's assumption of constant GDP. For instance, the average labor income declines 9 percent for the working-age population, mainly driven by the services sector, which accounts for more than 60 percent of total employment. These two effects produce a reduction in the amount that employed individuals contribute to total family income.

It is important to highlight that labor income is the most important component of total family income.[1] Thus, a decrease in the labor income translates into a reduction in the family's total welfare given that there are no changes in non-labor income components that could compensate for this variation. Under the assumption of constant prices, it is expected that an increase in the headcount poverty rate will be seen, as shown in table 7.9.

Figure 7.3: Employment Structure before and after Changes in Population

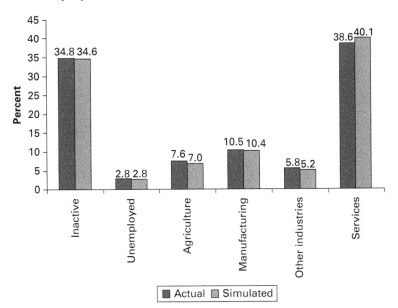

Table 7.9: Impacts of Changes in Population Structure on Incidence of Poverty

	Poverty headcount rate		
	Actual	Projected	Change
Urban	43.7	46.7	3.0
Rural	54.8	57.8	3.1
Total	47.6	50.4	2.8

Simulating Combined Changes in GDP and Labor Market Status

This exercise lifts the assumption that there is no relationship between GDP and the labor market. Therefore, *output-employment elasticities* are necessary to produce proper inputs for the simulation. First, growth rates for total and economic sector GDP in real terms are available. Different elasticities also allow the total number of unemployed, active, inactive, and employed individuals to be calculated by economic sector. The method explained in "Generating Total and Sector Changes in Employment and Labor Force Participation Data" in chapter 4 is used.

101

For instance, we want to project the population employed in services. The baseline number of people employed in this sector is 26.9 million (table 7.2). The output-employment elasticity for services is 0.80, meaning that an increase of 1 percent in services' GDP produces a 0.80 percent increase in total employment in services. We also have the projected percentage change in GDP in services (10 percent, from table 7.2). Thus;

$$\Delta\% \ Emp^S_{t1/t0} = 0.8 \times 10\% = 8\%$$

$$Emp^S_{t1} = 26.9 \times (1+8\%) = 29.07 \ \text{million people}$$

Repeating this same calculation for each economic sector and activity rate, and then calculating growth rates of shares, we obtain the Input 1 row of table 7.2. Under the assumption of no population growth and a 10 percent increase in total GDP, few people decide to leave the labor force, thereby producing a slight decrease in the activity rate. However, those who remain active face a significant increase in the employment rate and a reduction in the unemployment rate. Agriculture is the only sector that reduces its demand for workers and the services sector demand for workers increases the most.

It is not easy to predict the poverty impact when all these different effects are working together. On the one hand, the first exercise showed that growth in total and sectoral GDP produces a shift to the right of the distribution curve, which decreases poverty when everything else is kept constant.[2] On the other hand, the second exercise shows that a shift between employment sectors affects the shape of the distribution and could produce an increase in poverty when everything else is kept constant.[3] It is difficult to determine ahead of time which of these forces will dominate or if they are going to offset or reinforce each other.

After loading these inputs into the ADePT Simulation Module with the relative option for employment growth rates, the poverty headcount rate declines by 3.4 percentage points (table 7.10).

As mentioned, different forces produce different impacts on the income distribution; these different impacts could be captured by using the growth-redistribution decomposition of headcount poverty change. Figure 7.4 shows that the growth component is responsible for most of the reduction in poverty in the total economy and in both areas. However, this positive effect is partially offset by the change in the shape of the distribution (redistribution component), but only in rural areas.

Table 7.10: Impacts of Labor Market Changes on Incidence of Poverty

| | Poverty headcount rate | | |
	Actual	Projected	Change
Urban	43.7	40.0	−3.6
Rural	54.8	51.8	−3.0
Total	47.6	44.2	−3.4

Figure 7.4: Growth and Redistribution Impacts by Area

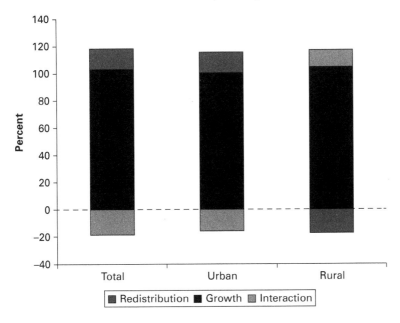

Notes

1. In this sample, it represents 82 percent of total family income.
2. We make the analogy with the first exercise because we are replicating the same GDP growth inputs in this first subsection. However, different growth rates of sectoral GDP may also affect the shape of the distribution.
3. Note this impact on the shape of the distribution curve depends on which economic sectors are shrinking and which are expanding.

Reference

Datt, G., and M. Ravallion. 1992. "Growth and Redistribution Components of Changes in Poverty Measures: A Decomposition with Applications to Brazil and India in the 1980s." *Journal of Development Economics* 38: 275–96.

Glossary

activity rate: The ratio of the labor force population to the total population.

activity-output elasticity: The ratio of the percentage change of the activity rate to the percentage change of total GDP in the same year.

baseline year: The last available release of a household or labor force survey in a country. For instance, if the last available Household Income and Expenditure Survey (HIES) in a country is 2006, then the baseline year is 2006.

computable general equilibrium model (CGE): A completely specified model of an economy or a region, including all production activities, factors, and institutions, and the modeling of all markets and macroeconomic components, such as investment and savings, balance of payments, and government budget. A CGE offers a comprehensive way of modeling the overall impact of policy changes on the economy. These models incorporate many economic linkages and can be used to try to explain medium- to long-term trends and structural responses to changes in development policy.

employment-output elasticity: The ratio of the percentage change in a sector's employment (for instance, manufacturing) to the percentage change in the same sector's GDP.

growth incidence curve (GIC): Indicates the growth rate in income or consumption between two points in time at each percentile of the distribution. More specifically, comparing two dates, $t-1$ and t, the growth rate (g) in income of the pth quantile is $gt(p) = [yt(p)/yt-1(p)]-1$.

growth rate: The percentage change between the baseline year (t_0) and projected year (t_1). Formally,

$$\Delta x = \frac{x_{t1} - x_{t0}}{x_{t0}},$$

in which x could be any macroeconomic input such as population, total GDP, or employment, among others. For instance, assume the assessment of the impact of a macro shock in 2013 for a country. The growth rate input of total output (GDP) is defined between 2006 and 2013 as

$$\Delta GDP = \frac{GDP13 - GDP06}{GDP06}.$$

labor force: Consists of individuals who belong to the working population and are employed or unemployed.

macroeconomic data (macrodata): The set of macroeconomic variables used as inputs in the microsimulation such as total value of the gross domestic product (GDP), GDP by economic sector, and labor market indicators such as total employment and by economic sector, unemployment rate, and out of labor force.

macroeconomic projection: The projected growth rate for each macroeconomic data element such as GDP or employment by economic sector, unemployment rate, and population projections, among others.

macroeconomic shock: An unexpected event that affects an economy's macroeconomic growth, either positively or negatively.

macro-linkage: A vector of aggregate employment and GDP variables used to shock a micro-household-level dataset, or to target the aggregate solution values of a micro model.

microeconomic data (microdata): The last available Household Income and Expenditure Survey or Labor Force Survey collected in the country.

multinomial logit model: An extension of the binary logit model when the unordered response has more than two outcomes. An example of unordered multinomial response is the occupation choice in which an individual chooses an employment status from the group of choices: inactive, unemployed, or employed in one particular economic sector; and the labeling of the choices is arbitrary.

poverty line: A cut-off point separating the poor from the non-poor.

remittances: Transfers in kind or in cash received from abroad by households.

scenario 1: Represents the behavior of the economy when it remains on trend (that is, **benchmark**) for a year, or any macroeconomic projection for a particular year.

scenario 2: Represents how the economy would react if there is a macroeconomic shock in the same year as in scenario 1, or any macroeconomic projection for any other year.

total employment: The sum of the total working population employed in different sectors.

transition matrix: Measures the absolute size of the impact of the macroeconomic projection among households, which, in some cases, is large enough to shift them to a lower or higher income decile, or in other cases is relatively small so the household's relative position does not change.

Additional References

Ajwad, M. I., M. Aran, M. Azam, and J. Hentschel. 2013. "A Methodology Note on the Employment and Welfare Impacts of the 2007–08 Financial Crisis." Research Paper 1303, Development Analytics, Oxford, U.K.

Alatas, V., and F. Bourguignon. 2005. "The Evolution of Income Distribution during Indonesia's Fast Growth, 1980–96." In *The Microeconomics of Income Distribution Dynamics in East Asia and Latin America*, edited by F. Bourguignon, F. Ferreira, and N. Lustig. Washington, DC: Oxford University Press and World Bank.

Beach, C. 1989. "Dollars and Dreams: A Reduced Middle Class? Alternative Explanations." *Journal of Human Resources* 24 (1): 162–93.

Blackburn, M., and D. Bloom. 1987. "Earnings and Income Inequality in the United States." *Population Development Review* 13 (4): 575–609.

Bourguignon, F., M. Bussolo, and L. Pereira da Silva. 2008. "The Impact of Macroeconomic Policies on Poverty and Income Distribution: Macro-Micro Evaluation Techniques and Tools." In *The Impact of Economic Policies on Poverty and Income Distribution: Macro-Micro Evaluation Techniques and Tools*, edited by F. Bourguignon and L. Pereira da Silva. Washington, DC: World Bank and Oxford University Press.

Bourguignon, F., and F. Ferreira. 2003. "Ex-ante Evaluation of Policy Reforms Using Behavioral Models." In *The Impact of Economic Policies on Poverty and Income Distribution: Macro-Micro Evaluation Techniques and Tools*, edited by F. Bourguignon and L. Pereira da Silva. Washington, DC: World Bank and Oxford University Press.

———. 2005. "Decomposing Changes in the Distribution of Household Incomes: Methodological Aspects." In *The Microeconomics of Income Distribution Dynamics in East Asia and Latin America*, edited by F. Bourguignon, F. Ferreira, and N. Lustig. Washington, DC: Oxford University Press and World Bank.

Bourguignon, F., M. Fournier, and M. Gurgand. 2007. "Selection Bias Corrections Based on the Multinomial Logit Model: Monte Carlo Comparisons." *Journal of Economic Surveys* 21 (1): 174–205.

Bourguignon, F., A. S. Robilliard, and S. Robinson. 2005. "Representative versus Real Households in the Macroeconomic Modeling of Inequality." In *Frontiers in Applied General Equilibrium Modeling: In Honor of Herbert Scarf*, edited by T. J. Kehoe, T. N. Srinivasan, and J. Whalley. Cambridge, U.K.: Cambridge University Press.

Bourguignon, F., and A. Spadaro. 2006. "Microsimulation as a Tool for Evaluating Redistribution Policies." *Journal of Economic Inequality* 4 (1): 77–106.

Burkhauser, R., A. Crews, A. Daly, and S. Jenkins. 1999. "Testing the Significance of Income Distribution Changes over the 1980s Business Cycle: A Cross-National Comparison." *Journal of Applied Econometrics* 14 (3): 253–72.

Bussolo, M., J. Lay, D. Medvedev, and D. van der Mensbrugghe. 2008. "Trade Options for Latin America: A Poverty Assessment Using a Top-Down Macro-Micro Modeling Framework." In *The Impact of Macroeconomic Policies on Poverty and Income Distribution: Macro-Micro Evaluation Techniques and Tools*, edited by F. Bourguginon, M. Bussolo, and L. Pereira da Silva. Washington, DC: World Bank.

Cho, Y., and D. Newhouse. 2010. "How Did the Great Recession Affect Different Types of Workers? Evidence from 17 Middle-Income Countries." Policy Research Working Paper 5636, World Bank, Washington, DC.

Deaton, A. 2001. Participation in a Panel Discussion in the International Monetary Fund–sponsored conference on "Macroeconomic Policies and Poverty Reduction." April 13, Washington, DC.

Ferreira, F., P. Leite, L. Pereira da Silva, and P. Picchetti. 2008. "Can the Distributional Impacts of Macroeconomic Shocks Be Predicted? A Comparison of Top-Down Macro-Micro Models with Historical Data for Brazil." In *The Impact of Macroeconomic Policies on Poverty and Income Distribution: Macro-Micro Evaluation Techniques and Tools*, edited by

F. Bourguignon, M. Bussolo, and L. Pereira da Silva. Washington, DC: World Bank.

Ganuza, E., S. Morley, S. Robinson, V. Piñeiro, and R. Vos. 2006. "Are Export Promotion and Trade Liberalization Good for Latin America's Poor? A Comparative Macro-Micro CGE Analysis." In *Who Gains from Free Trade? Export-Led Growth, Income Distribution and Poverty in Latin America*, edited by R. Vos, E. Ganuza, S. Morley, and S. Robinson. London and New York: Routledge.

Ganuza, E., R. Paes de Barros, and R. Vos. 2002. "Labour Market Adjustment, Poverty and Inequality during Liberalization." In *Economic Liberalization, Distribution and Poverty: Latin America in the 1990s*, edited by R. Vos, L. Taylor, and R. Paes de Barros. Cheltenham, U.K.: Edward Elgar.

Habib, B., A. Narayan, S. Olivieri, and C. Sánchez-Páramo. 2010a. "Assessing Ex Ante the Poverty and Distributional Impact of the Global Crisis in a Developing Country: A Micro-simulation Approach with Application to Bangladesh." Policy Research Working Paper 5238, World Bank, Washington, DC.

———. 2010b. "Assessing Poverty and Distributional Impacts of the Global Crisis in the Philippines: A Microsimulation Approach." Policy Research Working Paper 5286, World Bank, Washington, DC.

———. 2010c. "The Impact of the Financial Crisis on Poverty and Income Distribution: Insights from Simulations in Selected Countries." PREM Economic Premise 7, World Bank, Washington, DC.

———. 2012. "Assessing the Poverty and Distributional Impacts of the Financial Crisis with Microsimulations: An Overview of Country Studies." In *Knowing, When You Do Not Know: Simulating the Poverty and Distributional Impacts of an Economic Crisis*, edited by A. Narayan and C. Sánchez-Páramo. Washington, DC: World Bank.

Hallward-Driemeier, M., B. Rijkers, and A. Waxman. 2011. "Ladies First? Firm-Level Evidence on the Labor Impacts of the East Asian Crisis." Policy Research Working Paper 5789, World Bank, Washington, DC.

Jenkins, S. 1995. "Did the Middle Class Shrink during the 1980s? UK Evidence from Kernel Density Estimates." *Economics Letters* 49 (4): 407–13.

Kannan, P. 2009. "The Lingering Effects of Financial Crises." VoxEU website. http://www.voxeu.org/index.php?q=node/4232.

———, A. Scott, and M. Terrones. 2009. "From Recession to Recovery: A Long and Hard Road." VoxEU website. http://www.voxeu.org/index.php?q=node/3534.

Levy, F., and R. Murnane. 1992. "U.S. Earnings Levels and Earnings Inequality: A Review of Recent Trends and Proposed Explanations." *Journal of Economic Literature* 30 (3): 1333–81.

MacFadden, D. 1974. "Conditional Logit Analysis of Qualitative Choice Behavior." In *Frontiers in Econometrics*, edited by Paul Zarembka. New York: Academic Press.

Mincer, J. 1974. *Schooling, Experience and Earnings.* New York: Columbia University Press for National Bureau of Economic Research.

Paci, P., B. Rijkers, and A. Revenga. 2009. "Coping with Crisis: Why and How to Protect Employment and Earnings." Policy Research Working Paper 5094, World Bank, Washington, DC.

Paci, P., B. Rijkers, and A. Seinaert. 2008. "Crunch Time in the Developing World Too? Policy Options for Dealing with the Potential Poverty and Distributional Impact of the Financial Crisis." Poverty Reduction Group Policy Brief, World Bank, Washington, DC.

Paci, P., and M. Sasin. 2009. "Making Work Pay in Bangladesh: Employment, Growth, and Poverty Reduction." World Bank Directions in Development: Poverty.

Ravallion, M. 2009. "The Crisis and the World's Poorest." *Development Outreach* 11 (3): 16–18.

———. 2009. "The Developing World's Bulging (but Vulnerable) Middle Class." Policy Research Working Paper 4816, World Bank, Washington, DC.

Sabarwal, S., N. Sinha, and M. Buvinic. 2010. "How Do Women Weather Economic Shocks? What We Know." PREM Economic Premise 46, World Bank, Washington, DC.

Train, K., and W. Wilson. 2008. "Estimation on Stated-Preference Experiments Constructed from Revealed-Preference Choices." *Transportation Research Part B: Methodological* 42 (3): 191–203.

Turk, C., and A. Mason. 2009. "Impacts of the Economic Crisis in East Asia: Findings from Qualitative Monitoring in Five Countries." Discussion Draft, World Bank, Washington, DC.

Vos, R., L. Taylor, and R. Paes de Barro, eds. 2002. *Economic Liberalization, Distribution and Poverty. Latin America in the 1990s.* Northampton, Massachusetts: Edward Elgar.

Wittenberg, M. 2010. "An Introduction to Maximum Entropy and Minimum Cross-Entropy Estimation Using Stata." *Stata Journal* 10 (3): 315–30.

Wooldridge, J. 2002. *Econometric Analysis of Cross Section and Panel Data.* Cambridge, Massachusetts: MIT Press.

World Bank. 2008. "Poverty Assessment for Bangladesh: Creating Opportunities and Bridging the East-West Divide." Report No. 44321-BD, World Bank, Washington, DC.

———. 2009a. "Global Economic Crisis and Household Vulnerability in the Philippines: Potential Impacts and Policy Responses." East Asia Human Development Group, World Bank, Washington, DC.

———. 2009b. "Sailing Through Stormy Waters. Philippines Quarterly Update." World Bank, Washington, DC.

———. 2009c. "Welfare Impact of Rising Food Prices in South Asian Countries." Policy Note, South Asia Economic Policy and Poverty Unit, World Bank, Washington, DC.

———. 2010. "Recent Trends and Forecasts of Poverty in Mexico: A Poverty Note." Unpublished, Latin America and the Caribbean Region, World Bank, Washington, DC.

Index

Figures, notes, and tables are indicated by italic *f*, *n*, and *t*, respectively.